Skye Birds

An illustrated guide to the birds of Skye

and where to find them

R.L.McMILLAN

Illustrated by Jean Thomas

With colour photographs by the author and M. Benson

Published by skye-birds.com, Elgol, Isle of Skye

Skye Birds

Contents

First edition 2005
Second edition 2009

Published by skye-birds.com, Elgol, Broadford, Isle of Skye IV49 9BL

Text Copyright © R.L. McMillan 2009
Illustrations Copyright © Jean Thomas 2009
All photographs Copyright © to individual photographers

A CIP catalogue for this book is available from the British Library

ISBN 0 9550253 0 3

Printed in Great Britain by Strath Print, Broadford, Isle of Skye **www.strathprint.co.uk**

Front Cover - White-tailed Eagle near Portree © R.L. McMillan.

Acknowledgements

The late Jimmy Bayne from Dunblane stimulated my interest in birds over 45 years ago and introduced me to Skye. Many hours were spent in the library of the Scottish Ornithologists' Club when it was in Regents Terrace, Edinburgh and I am extremely grateful to all the staff for their support. Dr Francis Celoria's unpublished biography of the Rev. Hugh Macpherson was a fascinating source of reference. Andrew Currie provided support and ready access to a wealth of information which has been assiduously gathered over the years, some of it probably salvaged from inevitable destruction. Many individuals have contributed records to the Scottish Bird Report and the Highland Bird Reports which are reproduced here. I am grateful to Colin Crooke, the former Highland Recorder, for providing access to unpublished data. The Highland Bird Report under the stewardship of recorder Alistair McNee is setting a high standard which should continue to stimulate interest in local recording. A number of individuals have provided me with access to unpublished data including the Dix family, Bruce Philp, Ted Gerrard, Keith Miller, Neil Roberts, Crawford Godfrey, Roger Cottis, Kate Nellist and Ken Crane for which I am extremely grateful. Many individuals are now submitting records through the web site skye-birds.com and this is an ideal way of communicating to those living on the island, as well as to visitors, what species they are likely to see and where to see them. It is encouraging that there seems to be a growing band of observers resident on Skye who are keenly recording, which augers extremely well for the future.

I am extremely grateful to Jean Thomas of the Little Gallery, Portnalong, for the use of her etchings and line drawings which illustrate the species list. The photographs of Loch Coruisk, Elgol, and the Torrin crofting scene, are in the care of the Elgol and Torrin Historical Society and are reproduced with the permission of Eric G. Meadows. The portrait of the Rev. Hugh Macpherson is reproduced with the permission of the Carlisle Natural History Society. The portrait of Seton Gordon is reproduced with the permission of Dr. Adam Watson. Other photographs have been kindly provided by Martin Benson.

Finally, Kate Nellist has greatly assisted with proof reading and provided extremely helpful advice on lay-out in the 1st edition. John Phillips kindly proof-read the 2nd edition.

Foreword to Second Edition

The publication of Skye Birds was self-funded and the initial print run of 1500 was sold by early 2009. Because of the volume of records which have been submitted since, including some new species, it was decided that rather than do a straight reprint, the systematic species list would be updated, as would be the photographs and we would also update the cover. As well as gaining increasing local support, the website www.skye-birds.com is extensively used by visitors which helps to keep everyone up to date with what is being seen on the island and neighbouring areas. All records of note are passed to the Highland Recorder and therefore enter our regional and national databases – your records are important so please continue to support the site.

Bob McMillan
Elgol,
March, 2009.

INTRODUCTION

Islands hold a unique fascination and I still recall vivid memories of my first trip to Skye over 40 years ago. Born in landlocked Perthshire, the sea had tremendous pulling power, and visions of my first Skye campsite overlooking Staffin Bay can be instantly recalled. My older companions had introduced me to natural history, although on that holiday we spent a great deal of time exploring the Quiraing, and fishing for lythe off the rocks at Staffin, all in glorious September sunshine. In the following years the Cuillin were a major passion, then later, more leisurely exploration of distant corners of Sleat and Minginish. Skye has a habit of drawing you back and after many holidays and visits we managed to find a house in Elgol a few years ago, where we now live permanently. Perched on the Atlantic edge, Elgol embraces all of Skye's elements, particularly the sea, the majestic Cuillin, and wild, sometimes frightening weather. Add to that a garden bird list which includes Red-throated Diver, Peregrine, White-tailed Eagle, Great Skua, Twite, Waxwing and Lapland Bunting, for a keen bird watcher, it's not a bad place to be.

Probably more has been written about Skye than any other island in Scotland – the grandeur of the Cuillin – the wonderful coastline and seascapes – the geology – the history – the myths and legends – the people – where to walk – where to climb – the list is endless. Conversely, little has been written about Skye's natural history, and a number of commentators have summarily dismissed Skye as a bit of an ornithological backwater, important for eagles but not much more. This partly explains why it is one of the few Scottish islands for which there is no dedicated guide book. It should be stressed however, that this publication is not a new idea. For many years Andrew Currie has enlightened readers of the West Highland Free Press with his regular column on natural history and matters ornithological. In the 1980s Andrew set about gathering bird records to produce a booklet, but for a variety of personal reasons this ambition was not fulfilled. Andrew has very kindly passed me all his records, and this has contributed significantly to this volume.

You have to work hard for your birds on Skye, but the objective of this publication is to show that there is a much greater diversity of species than may have been previously realised; to produce a species list which might serve as a baseline for the future; to give some pointers to visitors on the best places to watch birds, and to provide some stimulus to locals to go and find what may always have been on their doorsteps.

At the beginning of the 20th century, J. A. Harvie-Brown, a gentleman ornithologist from Stirlingshire, embarked on the massive task of producing regional reference works on the Fauna of Scotland. In 1904 he produced A Fauna of the North West Highlands and Skye, the bulk of the records for Skye having been provided by the Rev. Hugh Alexander Macpherson from Glendale. This work still sets the historical benchmark, and 100 years on, it is time to bring the record up to date.

1. SKYE – THE TOPOGRAPHY AND HABITATS

Skye is the largest and most northerly of the Inner Hebrides island group. Its eastern shore is separated from the mainland by Loch Alsh, the 700 metre gap now spanned by the new Skye Bridge (now toll-free!). At its narrowest point at Kylerhea, a mere 500 metres separates Skye from the mainland, a former crossing point for cattle which were destined for markets further south and now a popular summer ferry point. In the context of bird distribution this physical proximity to the mainland must be borne in mind. Water is a major barrier which can prevent the spread and distribution of species, but it is hardly applicable in the context of Skye. It is therefore reasonable to assume that most species which are established in the north-west coast of Scotland should find a niche in Skye. There has been much talk in the historical past about native sub-species in Skye, but given such proximity to the mainland, this seems unlikely.

Several other islands lie close to Skye, and are regarded as part of the main island group for the purposes of this reference book. The largest of these is Raasay, which from an ornithological perspective has been relatively well documented. Other islands include Scalpay, South Rona and Soay, all of which are relatively unexplored. For a number of years Pabay was owned by an active bird ringer. Smaller islands are scattered round the coast. Many of these are important for birds, especially those in the north-west of the island such as the Ascribs, Fladda-chùain, and Isay which have breeding seabirds and wintering geese.

The main island is 78 kilometres long from Point of Sleat to Rubha Hunish, and at its widest point, 67 kilometres from east to west. However, the coastline is a staggering 570 kilometres in length, hence it is extremely difficult to escape the sea – it is said that on Skye it is impossible to be at any point more that 8 kilometres from the coast. There are two Gaelic names for Skye, Eilean a' Cheo, the isle of the mist, and Eilean Sgiathanach, because it rests upon the wind-swept sea like a mighty bird with outstretched pinions. In the context of this book the latter is highly appropriate, each wing representing one of the long promontories which spring from a central body, the majestic mountain mass of the Cuillin. More than a dozen fiordic sea lochs split the promontories, creating a coastline which is long and varied. It therefore may not be surprising that many of the birdwatching locations suggested later are on the coast. It is also worth noting that each of the long promontories creates opportunities for sea watching which have hardly been exploited. Add to that the pleasure of watching birds in some of the most spectacular scenery in Britain, then it is an opportunity worth taking.

As much as Skye has a reputation for scenery, it also has a reputation for weather. Exposed to oceanic influences, it is almost inevitable that Skye has high rainfall, over 300 centimetres annually in the heart of the Cuillin. However, rainfall figures vary significantly throughout the island, much dependent on the influence of the mountains. Even on the Strathaird peninsula, it can be dry at Elgol but lashing with rain at the head of Loch Slapin only a few miles away. The north of the island also has significantly less rain than the south. Wind is a major factor and gales tend to reach major velocity in the winter months. However, an understanding of weather systems is critically important for bird watching. If winds are lashing in from the north, birds will inevitably seek shelter along south-facing coasts and bays. When a south-westerly is blowing in the south of Skye, Broadford Bay is well worth a look. Weather movements of birds are complex, and at times when the weather closes in, the temptation is to retreat to a warm fire. This is often the time to get out and about. Some of the best days birding in Skye have been on days of strong westerlies in May, when birds were driven in to areas such as Loch Slapin, seeking shelter during their northward migration. Sea watchers have long recognised that their best days are often the roughest days. It is perhaps best to think of Skye as a series of microclimates, as, even on the darkest days, the sun may be shining somewhere on the island. As Derek Cooper suggests, planning a holiday on Skye is as risky as playing Russian roulette. For many, it is the extremes of the weather and its interplay with the landscape which draws them back to Skye time and again.

The topography of Skye has been shaped by its geology and the island continues to be a focus for geological research. It is significant that amongst the many Sites of Special Scientific Interest (SSSIs) on Skye, most have been designated for geological purposes. The Cuillin Hills and the Trotternish Ridge are designated SSSIs, and substantial areas around both have been designated as National Scenic Areas (NSAs). It is not the purpose here to explain the complex geology as this is amply explained elsewhere. However, as many of the habitats are a direct result of the geology, it is important to provide a brief explanation.

Loch Coruisk from the summit of Sgurr na Stri © Eric G Meadows

The landscape is dominated by the Cuillin, a central volcano from which lavas flowed northwards, forming the Duirinish and Waternish peninsulas and part of Trotternish. The main Cuillin and Blaven ridges are carved from coarse-grained rock known as gabbro, whilst the more gentle but steep sloping 'red hills' nearby were cut from granite formed deep within the volcano. The hard volcanic rock helped to protect more friable underlying layers of sandstone, limestone and clays, which outcrop near the shore, especially along the north-east coast of the island. These same rocks comprise part of Raasay and also extend to the Broadford area and Strathaird. The sandstone, shales and limestone provide better soils and this has influenced patterns of settlement. Conversely, the Sleat peninsula comprises mostly Torridonian red sandstone and gneiss, or granite, amongst the oldest rocks in Britain. All the rocks of Skye were heavily eroded by glaciers during the Ice Age, creating great corries, and the spectacular serrated ridges in the Cuillin. Glaciers flowed out, gouging valleys and sea lochs such as Glen Drynoch, Loch Ainort and Loch Scavaig. Another glacier flowed south-westwards to the Sound of Sleat, effectively separating Skye from the mainland. The work of ice is responsible for the deep U shaped valleys and deep sea lochs so typical of the landscape of Skye.

The Old Man of Storr © John Phillips

The Trotternish Ridge is an example of a landslip, apparently the largest in Britain, resulting from the retreat of the ice which left vertical walls of eroded lavas sitting on unstable weak clays, the resulting collapse creating yet another unique landscape. Following the departure of the ice, the sea has continued to modify the coastline, much of which consists of cliffs, often spectacular in themselves. Though man has further changed the landscape, human influences on the habitats are perhaps less profound than in many

11

other areas of the country. However, they are none the less important, and remain constant and dynamic in terms of their influence on bird life. Whilst the interrelationship between man and wildlife has historically been beneficial on the island, it has often been by accident rather than design, and there is a need for a much fuller understanding of the interdependencies. Significant changes in the distribution of certain species have occurred in the last 20 years, some positive in terms of improved status, but on the negative side a number of species have been lost. This is an indication of how fragile and dynamic the balance is. Some of these issues will be explored later, but in the first instance it is best to take a broad-brush look at the habitats which are critical for many of these species.

Habitats have been categorised under five general heads and follow the approach adopted in the recently published *Skye and Lochalsh Biodiversity Action Plan* (2003).

Sea and Coast

Because of the influence of the North Atlantic drift, the water temperatures round the coast of Skye are significantly higher than the east coast of Scotland. Coastal water systems are therefore mostly frost free. Species such as Greenshank and Grey Wagtail therefore winter in reasonable numbers. The open sea contains some of the deepest underwater cliffs in Scotland, plunging to depths of over 100 metres relatively close inshore. Many of the coastal cliffs, though steep and precipitous, are unsuitable for large concentrations of seabirds, but there is continued expansion of important breeding populations of Fulmar, Shag and Black Guillemot. These species exploit both inshore and offshore feeding opportunities along with Guillemots, Razorbills, Kittiwakes and other gulls. In spring and autumn there are huge flocks of Guillemots, Razorbills and Manx Shearwaters offshore, many from the large colonies on nearby Rum, Canna and the Shiants. The importance of the deep water feeding available in the north of Skye was identified during a ship-based survey in 1986 (Benn *et al.* 1988), but it appears that the southern part of Skye still requires proper assessment. There is certainly evidence that Guillemots and Razorbills from colonies in the north-west of Scotland, numbering 120,000+, disperse south through the Minches into the Sea of Hebrides in response to feeding opportunities. As much of the coastline is rocky, it provides limited opportunities for feeding waders. Wildfowl and divers tend to concentrate in shallower bays and sea lochs. As a consequence these species are more common on the more sheltered eastern side of the island, and at the head of sea lochs. A number of these locations feature in a later chapter on suggested sites to watch birds. Probably the most important site is the Broadford Bay complex, a stopover point for migrating waders, which in winter contains significant numbers of Great Northern Divers, Slavonian Grebes and Red-breasted Mergansers. In recent years it has also been discovered that Lochs Slapin and Scavaig are important for wintering Black-throated Divers, with counts of 30+, and Skye may provide a wintering ground for up to 20% of the total UK breeding population.

Freshwater

The topography and high rainfall determines that the majority of rivers are short and fast-flowing with rapid run off. River systems provide suitable breeding habitat for Grey Wagtails, Dippers and Common Sandpipers. Many of the lochs are small and nutrient poor, the best being Loch Cill Chriosd, Loch Mealt and Loch Suardal. A number are breeding haunts for Little Grebe, Mallard, Teal, and Tufted Duck. Red-throated Divers have expanded their range during the last 30 years and the population of c50 pairs appears to have good productivity. Moorhen continue to breed in small numbers though the Coot has not bred for at least 25 years. Despite being mostly frost free, the lochs hold very few species in winter apart from a small population of Whooper Swans and Goldeneye. A number of lochs have reedy fringes which remain suitable for breeding Reed Bunting though the population appears to be decreasing. A small *Phragmites* bed at Loch Cill Chriosd contains a summer roost of Swallows and Pied Wagtails. Waterside margins and pools are also important for breeding Snipe and Greenshank.

In-bye Croft and Farm Land

The majority of crofts on Skye are between two and five hectares in size. Mainly located on the coastal fringes, historically on the most fertile parts of the island, most have been cultivated over a long period of time with a variety of crops. Historically this is one of the most biologically diverse habitats supporting a wide range of species which in the past has included Corn Bunting, Yellowhammer, Reed Bunting, Linnet and Twite. Kenneth Richmond (1968) wrote 'in summer the sedgy, meadowsweet pastures near

Species rich pastures at Elgol in 1953 with the Cuillin Ridge in the background © Eric G Meadows

Broadford are alive with Corn Buntings, Corncrakes and Twite, in winter crowded with flocks of Greenfinches, Siskins and other finches.' However, with the recent changes in crofting practice, the landscape has become much less diverse, and there is much greater concentration on sheep and livestock, with a tendency in some areas towards overgrazing. Equally, many crofting areas are underused or neglected. Where proper management and traditional practices remain in place, this sits well in supporting a range of species including Corncrake and Twite. However, it has to be recognised that changes in crofting practices in the last 25 years have probably led to the disappearance of Corn Bunting and a significant reduction in range of Reed Bunting, Linnet and Yellowhammer. Waders such as Lapwing and Curlew were never over abundant on Skye but there has been a notable decrease in Lapwing numbers from areas of improved pasture. Good management of croft lands is beneficial for birds, and a variety of projects and schemes are available to encourage biodiversity.

Woodland

There are few natural or semi-natural woodlands remaining on Skye and these tend to be concentrated in the south of the island. In particular these include upland birch, ash and oakwood communities, some of the best examples being at Mudalach, Kinloch, and Coille Dalavil as well as remnants in other corners of Sleat and Strath. Many of these woodlands are seriously undergrazed which inhibits any regeneration. Other coastal remnants have been protected because they are relatively inaccessible. There are no native pinewoods on Skye. There are interesting mixed woodlands, albeit containing some exotics, at Armadale, around Portree and Dunvegan. A number of these are associated with formal planting round some of the larger houses. Many of these woodlands have yet to be the subject of proper ornithological surveys. Whilst a number of typical species have been recorded, including Redstart, Tree Pipit, Spotted Flycatcher and Wood Warbler, their distribution and density is as yet a mystery. Whilst there are records of Pied Flycatcher on Skye, as far as can be established there has been no breeding record, though birds have been recorded during the breeding season.

Whilst a small number of softwood plantations were planted on Skye and Raasay at the end of the 19th century, the main objective was probably to provide cover for game. The first commercial planting by the Forestry Commission started in 1932 at Glen Eynort and by 1947 some 538 hectares had been established. Major planting has taken place since the 1950s, and in the last 30 years a significant part of central Skye has been planted, amounting to a total of c14,000 hectares. Sitka Spruce and Lodgepole Pine account for at least 80% of all plantings. Much forestry is now under private ownership and management. A great deal has been written about the lack of biodiversity in such plantations, about problems of acidification and habitat destruction. In regard to the latter it would certainly appear that vast areas have been planted up with little cognisance of wildlife interest. Habitat once used by breeding Red-throated Divers, Greenshank, Dunlin and Golden

Plovers has probably disappeared. A great deal of recent planting however, was also on overgrazed upland habitats which were probably species poor, on wet ground with poor soils, and in extremely exposed positions. It is perhaps not surprising that the growth performance of many of these woodlands has been so poor that there are huge areas of stunted growth and die-back.

A typical Skye coniferous plantation © skye-birds.com

In the current climate it is ironic that much will never be commercially harvested. Conversely however, again more by accident than design, many of these forests provide a woodland mosaic which has been colonised by a whole range of species. Some of these woods teem with bird life, especially Redpolls, Siskins, Bullfinches, Coal Tits, Goldcrests, Chaffinches, Mistle and Song Thrushes. The Common Crossbill is now well established on Skye. Merlins have adapted to forest nesting. Hen Harriers use these forests extensively and it has only recently been discovered that there is a significant population on Skye. Throughout the systematic list which follows, reference is made to a number of species which now appear to be much more common than in historical times. Given the virtual absence of forest cover in north Skye 30 years ago, there seems little doubt that forest plantations have provided corridors along which species have moved, colonised, and expanded their range. Perhaps there is a need to think about how these areas might be better managed for wildlife, than simply brashed or cut for firewood, because many of the forests have no commercial value or are too difficult to harvest.

Much encouragement is being provided to plant native hardwoods, or to allow existing native woodlands to naturally regenerate. In terms of ornithological diversity this will clearly bring long-term benefits. Unfortunately there is already evidence that some native woodland plantations are failing to thrive and may have been inappropriately located.

Mountain and Moorland

It is the mountain landscapes, especially the Cuillin, which are an ever constant presence in most parts of Skye, and a continual influence on the weather, especially in the south of the island. In the north, the Trotternish ridge and the Quiraing can be equally spectacular. From a birding point of view however, both are relatively species poor. Both have also suffered as a result of over grazing, even at significant altitudes. The Cuillin mountain range is now designated as a Special Protection Area (SPA) for breeding Golden Eagles. Ptarmigan favour the Red Hills and the mountain mass between Kinloch, Kylerhea and Kyleakin, though their numbers may be in decline. Ring Ouzels breed in the Cuillin and Trotternish. Though Dotterel and Snow Bunting have been recorded in summer there is no evidence that they have bred. White-tailed Eagles have faired extremely well on Skye following the re-introduction programme and mountain and moorland habitats are extremely important for their long term survival and population expansion.

At lower altitudes the most widespread habitats include heather moorland, peatland and acidic grasslands. Oceanic influences, especially on the west coast, mean that these habitats extend to sea level. Much is managed as 'common grazings', mainly for sheep. Though in the past moorlands were managed for Red Grouse, there is only a small area in Sleat where this continues. Much heather moorland has either been overgrazed or badly damaged by inappropriate muirburning. It will be seen from the previous paragraphs that much of this habitat is now under commercial afforestation. Red Grouse continue to breed though their distribution is rather sparse. Snipe are common and although Golden Plovers are widely distributed, their breeding density is low. Lapwing and Curlew are surprisingly scarce. There is a good population of breeding Greenshank, probably higher than previously realised, and birds breed up to the 420 metre contour. The population of Hen Harriers breeding on Skye is also significant and though birds tend to nest in forest plantations much of their foraging for prey is over moorland and grasslands. Little is known of the Merlin population but it is thought to be well distributed. The main passerine species are Skylarks, Meadow Pipit, Stonechat and Whinchat.

2. PERCEPTIONS AND SOME CONSERVATION ISSUES

It should now be evident to those unfamiliar with Skye that this can be a harsh environment, and the forces of nature have left an indelible mark on the landscape. Any good soils are restricted to a few sheltered valleys and coastal edges where the vegetation is at risk from overgrazing by sheep or deer. These are not necessarily the richest of habitats for birds as is evident from the previous chapter. This perception may not be new:

> 'It now, as formerly, appears to me to be almost the poorest and least favoured of our Scottish Faunal Areas, both as regards species and in the paucity of individuals of many of them.' (Harvie-Brown, 1904)

> 'Topographically, Skye is magnificent, with its Cuillin, and the Quiraing, but from the point of view of wildlife it is somewhat disappointing.' (Fraser-Darling & Boyd 1964)

Until the designation of the Cuillin SPA for Golden Eagles there were no statutory sites on Skye designated for ornithological reasons. Whilst a number of Local Natural Heritage Sites appear in the Skye and Lochalsh Local Plan, these are under the broad head of 'Nature Conservation' rather than specifically for birds. From the perspective of both the statutory and voluntary organisations, it almost appears as if they are in accord with some of the founding fathers of natural history. Writing in 1968 Kenneth Richmond was one of the few individuals to suggest that Skye was far from being the relatively birdless island it often appeared to be at first

Adult Golden Eagle © skye-birds.com

sight. Certainly in comparison with other islands, Skye may not have the spectacular seabird colonies of the Shetlands or the Orkneys; it may not have the wintering wildfowl of Islay, and it does not have the breeding colonies of waders and wildfowl found on the machair lands of the Uists. Yet in terms of the diversity of its breeding species from both the 1968-72 *Atlas*, and the 1988-91 *Atlas*, Skye emerges very favourably. As far as wintering birds are concerned, again the 1981-83 *Winter Atlas* gives Skye a very favourable placing given its location. The Skye list currently stands at 244 species, a major limiting factor being the shortage of active birders, rather than the absence of rarities. In regard to species which are 'Red' listed as being of high conservation concern, 14 breed on Skye. A total of 65 species, which either breed or occur on passage or overwinter, are 'Amber' listed as being of medium conservation concern. It may already be evident, that some of the historical perspectives were slightly premature.

Skye is well placed to turn up North American vagrants, the best example being the breeding attempt by a pair of Spotted Sandpipers in 1975. Little is known of the occurrence of other unusual migrants and vagrants, and work requires to be done to identify potential hotspots. There is visible migration at a number of locations, and strong evidence that locations such as Broadford Bay are important re-fuelling points for migrating waders. Sea watching opportunities are extensive and totally unexploited. There is certainly no lack of opportunities for dedicated birders, and hard work will be well rewarded. The spectacular scenery of Skye provides a unique backcloth for wonderful days in the field.

Typical Crofting scene at Torrin in 1960 © Eric G Meadows

Some of the conservation issues have already been touched on, and they are not unique to the Island of Skye. Problems caused by muirburning, overgrazing and inappropriate planting have still to be overcome. The decline in traditional methods of crofting has had a deleterious effect on a number of passerine species. Corn Buntings have been extinct on the island for 25 years and the Yellowhammer is reduced to only a few pairs in Sleat. Linnet and Reed Bunting are significantly reduced from former levels. These changes

18

have occurred in the last 25 years, changes which may be irreversible, yet they have occurred with hardly a murmur of concern. Little brown birds don't always figure too high in our priorities!

Aquaculture has been developed extensively round the coast of Skye but no study has been carried out to assess its impact on birds. It certainly appears to benefit some species on the basis of the numbers of gulls, Shags and auks which are invariably found in the proximity of fish farm sites, exploiting either the surplus salmon feed or the shoals of small fish attracted by it.

When it comes to the conservation of birds of prey, sporting estates have had blood on their hands and those on Skye were no exception. The persecution still goes on in many areas, so it is perhaps fortunate that there is only one sporting estate remaining on the island and it appears to be more enlightened than most. The use of poisons to kill birds of prey, either directly or indirectly, is illegal, but unfortunately it is still widespread in Scotland. A Hen Harrier brood of 5 young was deliberately trampled to death in 2008 so Skye is not immune from the problem.

The most recent potential conservation threat, especially to birds of prey, is the development of wind farms. Experience on the Continent and in North America certainly suggests that large birds of prey such as eagles as well as other species including divers, are vulnerable to collision with turbines, especially those of the size proposed. There is a tremendous thrust towards such developments on so-called sustainable energy grounds. However where such sites impact upon high risk species of national conservation concern, political expediency must not be prioritised until adequate information has been obtained to determine where turbines and the associated infrastructure can be sensitively located, if at all. Those involved in gathering ornithological data have an important contribution to make in a process where environmental consultants, employed by the developers, may not always provide an independent and balanced view. The author has suggested elsewhere (McMillan, 2005) that there is a need for Scottish Natural Heritage to develop a coherent and robust policy which properly assesses all the risks. Edinbane and Ben Aketil windfarms have been approved despite a high collision risk for Golden Eagles and by the application of a scientific model which has been widely criticised. A requirement on the developers to check below the turbines for "strikes" could have helped to verify the model – no such requirement is in place.

3. ORNITHOLOGISTS, BIRDWATCHERS AND BIRDERS – A HISTORY

In an historical context it might be expected that some acknowledgement would be given to the contribution by the famous travellers to the West Highlands who included Thomas Pennant in 1772 and Dr Johnston in 1773. Their ornithological input however was relatively insignificant and the earlier work by Martin Martin (c1695) was more authoritative. The pioneering work of William MacGillivray established new boundaries in the scientific study of birds in the early 19th century. Though he was brought up on Harris there is little evidence that he spent much time on Skye or contributed to the early knowledge of the island's avifauna. Both the *Old* and the *New Statistical Accounts* can be useful sources of information. However, they are limited to the knowledge base of the local clergy, and it certainly appears that in most parishes in Skye, the clergy were preoccupied by more important ecclesiastical matters.

The first significant historical reference was *The Birds of the West of Scotland* by Robert Gray published in 1871. Gray was a member of the British Ornithologists' Union and had been Secretary of The Natural History Society of Glasgow. The volume was dedicated to the Rt. Hon. The Earl of Haddington who had obviously been a source of much of the information. Ornithology at the time was very much the preserve of 'gentlemen and aristocrats' who were also keen field sportsmen. Many also collected eggs and skins of birds, the latter being the normal method of bird identification. The work was the first attempt to document the birds of Scotland, albeit it concentrated mainly on the western parts. Gray certainly claimed that he had visited most parts of the west coast to collect information and there is evidence that he corresponded with a number of individuals on Skye, but little evidence that he actually visited. Macpherson (1886) certainly took the view that much of Gray's information had been provided by a Dr Dewar and Captain Cameron of Glen Brittle. In general terms estate owners and their gamekeepers would be the main sources of information, reliable or otherwise. As well as public collections of skins, mounted specimens, and eggs, large private collections would form a valuable source of material. Gray's work was a formidable achievement for the time, and was presented in the form of a systematic list of species. As well as providing common and Latin names, he consulted various sources and included Gaelic names. It also contains some graphic accounts of the perilous status of a number of vulnerable species at the time, particularly birds of prey. However, it appears that Gray failed to recognise that several of these species were on the verge of extinction through human persecution.

The most significant work published regarding the birds of Skye was *A Fauna of the North West Highlands and Skye* by J. A. Harvie-Brown and the Rev. H. A. Macpherson, which was published in 1904. At this time a series of *Fauna* were being published for different geographical areas of Scotland, the principle author being J.A. Harvie-Brown. Macpherson and Harvie-Brown had been friends and correspondents for 20 years. In respect of the Skye data, most had been collected by Macpherson who had died in 1901 at the age of 43 years. Macpherson made a unique contribution to our knowledge of the birds of Skye and is worthy of special mention here.

The Rev. Hugh Alexander Macpherson

Hugh Macpherson was born in Calcutta of Scottish parents; his father was from Aberdeen and his mother, a MacLeod, was thought to have Skye connections. Macpherson was educated at Oxford where his interest in natural history blossomed, although his studies for a degree in divinity seemed to stumble along. Macpherson's uncle, Sir John Macpherson MacLeod, bought the Glendale Estate in north-west Skye from the trustees of the MacLeod of MacLeod in 1852. Though Sir John added to the estate he is said to have visited it only once, and on his death in 1881 it was left to his nephew Hugh, something of a poisoned chalice as will later be apparent.

Rev. Hugh Alexander Macpherson © Carlisle Historical Society

There is no evidence that Hugh Macpherson had visited the estate prior to this time, but it certainly appeared that he immediately developed a love for the island and a passionate interest in the birds of Skye which was to continue until his death. Macpherson however, was never resident in Skye and on graduation assumed clerical duties in Carlisle and immediately dedicated himself to the ornithology of the surrounding district. Most of his holidays however were spent at Hamara Lodge in Glendale. In 1886 he published *The Birds of Cumberland.* It is a reflection on his writing productivity that in the same year he presented a paper on *The Birds of Skye, with special reference to the Parish of Duirinish* (Part 1) to the Royal Physical Society in Edinburgh, the first publication specific to the ornithology of Skye. Macpherson recorded 153 species including Nuthatch, Barred Warbler and Great Shearwater, which he claimed as new to the Hebrides. Other publications included *The Vertebrate Fauna of Lakeland* in 1892 and *A History of Fowling* in 1897. In 1899 Macpherson left the Carlisle area to take up an appointment at the Episcopal Church in Pitlochry. Unfortunately by this time he was in failing health. His chief wish had been to write a work on the vertebrata of Skye, perhaps the Part 2 of his earlier paper. Though much of the preparatory work had been carried out, he died before his ambition could be realised. His long time friend Harvie-Brown extended the posthumous honour of co-authorship on *The Fauna of the North West Highlands and Skye* when it was published in 1904. Though Harvie-Brown had the reputation for being meticulous, it should be noted that a number of Macpherson's records, submitted to *The Zoologist* following the publication of his 1886 paper, were omitted from this work.

Like others of his time, he had a huge collection of bird skins and these were presented to the Museum of Carlisle. Macpherson, as well as being a prolific gatherer of information, accurate and painstaking in his research, was also a dedicated field ornithologist as is evident from many of his records. Like Gray, many of his contacts were amongst the local estates but his list of species and detailed records was extremely comprehensive. It is evident from his diaries that his numerous contacts included fishermen, bird catchers, bird stuffers, gamekeepers, factors, and doubtless poachers (Celoria 2001). Though not a wealthy man, he probably gave rewards for providing information and reimbursement for specimens sent by rail and post. It also appeared that he supplied books and periodicals to 'working' men to encourage them to gather information on migration, arrival dates and uncommon birds. His estate factor regularly sent parcels of birds and eggs. There is also a letter from a gamekeeper in Broadford dated 20 November 1899, who wrote to thank Macpherson for bird books and who promised to look out for 'strange birds'. Though Macpherson was a member of the British Ornithologists' Union, he displayed many of the traits and characteristic of modern birders.

It is perhaps understandable that there was a bias of recording towards the north of the island, very few records being gathered from Sleat and Strath. However, in the context of Skye his work was a major achievement. Despite this, he remains little known on the island. Conversely, he is well remembered in Carlisle and in 2001 its Tullie House Museum put on a temporary exhibition commemorating the 100th anniversary of his death and celebrating the achievements of his life.

That Macpherson was so little known on Skye may reflect the fact that willingly or otherwise, he was a landowner. He inherited an estate which had been under the control of an absentee landlord and which was in turmoil. Probably because of his age, control of the estate was in the hands of trustees, including his brother William Macpherson, an advocate, and a Sheriff Norman Macpherson. Management of the estate was in the hands of a local Factor, who had a reputation as a petty tyrant and who forbade crofters from keeping dogs, and fenced off grazings. Crofters could barely scrape an existence from tiny landholdings. This eventually led in 1882 to the famous Glendale riots where soldiers, marines and the Glasgow Police had to be called to restore order. As a result three local crofters, 'the Glendale Martyrs', were imprisoned in Edinburgh. Throughout the West of Scotland there was major conflict between crofters, landowners and their factors which led to the Napier Commission, a major milestone in crofting rights. The discontent and disturbances slowly died down but left the estate, even to this day, with an unenviable reputation in what was a monumental period in Skye's history. How much of a distraction this was from Hugh's obsession with the local bird life, is difficult to assess, and on the basis of his prodigious writings it might appear that there was very little. However, when he wrote *Ornithological Notes from Skye* for *The Zoologist* of 1883 there was the following preamble:

'In justice to the fauna of Skye, it is right to say I had even less time to examine it than last year, owing to the presence of the Crofters Commission, and many other demands on my time.'

This is perhaps a slight understatement! It appears that on his death the estate was sold back to MacLeod of MacLeod. However, in 1903 it was purchased by the Congested Districts Boards, in effect the State, and has remained in local public ownership since that time. It is not the purpose here to make judgements on Macpherson's role in the running of the estate, bearing in mind that he was 24 years of age at the time of the riots, and the estate was managed by trustees. In an ornithological context however, nothing can take away from the fact that with regard to publications, articles, and notes in Journals such as *The Zoologist*, Macpherson wrote and discovered more about the birds of Skye than any individual before him, or any individual since.

As well as having a lesser knowledge of the south of the island, it is assumed that Macpherson never visited Raasay. The *Fauna* contains many references to Raasay which were provided either by Harvie-Brown or by others such as Lionel Hinxman from the Scottish Geological Survey, who was an accomplished ornithologist. Living on Raasay at the time was another member of the BOU, Charles Collier who in 1904 published a detailed account of the Birds of the Island of Raasay in *Ibis*. Collier was the shooting tenant and had been resident on the island for seven years between 1896 and 1902 and was therefore able to provide detailed information on winter visitors as well as the summer breeding populations. It is interesting to speculate why Macpherson and Collier, both members of the BOU, may have never met. Perhaps Macpherson did not regard Raasay as being part of Skye. Several others contributed to the Raasay bird record including a Mrs Gaskell who wrote an article in *The Scottish Naturalist* following a visit in 1916, and an expedition from the Armstrong College who gathered data in 1935. Following brief visits in 1936 and 1937 George W. Temperley produced a paper on *The Natural History of the Island of Raasay* published in *The Scottish Naturalist* in 1938, and which contained some comparative analysis with the previous records. As nothing further had been published in regard to the main island of Skye since 1904, it would certainly appear that in the late 1930s as much was known about Raasay as any other part of the island group. Meanwhile, another individual worthy of special mention had taken residence at Duntulm in the north of Skye.

Seton Gordon

Born in Aberdeen in 1886, Seton Gordon was an only child whose parents were extremely well connected, his father being the Town Clerk of Aberdeen and his mother, whose literary skills made her a favourite of Queen Victoria, became affectionately known as the 'Queen's Poetess'. Not only in terms of the Aberdeen connection, but in terms of social background, there was some similarity to Macpherson, but probably there, any similarity ends. Whilst Macpherson was very much a naturalist and collector of the Victorian era, Seton Gordon was an exploratory naturalist, mountaineer, photographer, and accomplished writer of the modern time, who ranged throughout Scotland and who possessed a wide range of interests and knowledge.

Seton Gordon at 90 in the Cairngorms
© *Adam Watson*

Seton Gordon's introduction to Skye was probably in 1914 and it is thought he visited the island on a number of occasions in the succeeding years. In 1925 the family had a holiday on the island for the first time, staying for several months, latterly at Duntulm Lodge. This proved the starting point for a lasting love affair with the island, its culture, history, its piping tradition, its people, and especially his beloved Cuillin. The family also became immersed in island social life. Prolonged annual visits were made until 1931 when the Gordons bought the former Kilmuir Manse and 70 acres, which following renovations, was re-named Upper Duntulm. This was to be home for the rest of his life, until he died at 90 years of age in 1977. For a full account of his life in Skye it is recommended that readers see the biography by Raymond Eagle published in 1991. On his death there were many fitting tributes, none less so than by Dr Adam Watson who as a 13 year old boy had met Seton Gordon and been inspired by him. Part of the obituary in *Scottish Birds* reads:

'As with many fine naturalists, most details within his exceptional experience will have died with him. He was a masterly describer of things in breadth, of incident, of anecdote. Detailed analytical research was not his way, and this is as true as his contributions on place names and history as on ornithology. However, analytical researchers and men interested in problems often fail to interest the layman, and seldom excite him as Gordon did for many. Future Scotsmen will read him when many of the analysts have been forgotten.'

In a publication of this nature, which relies on detailed information, this is the nub of the challenge, because although Seton Gordon kept copious notes of particular species he was studying, such as the Golden Eagle, he did not appear to keep many casual records. There is nothing this author would have enjoyed better than to have a chat with the 'grand old man', on his recollections of the birds of Skye, and this would inevitably have filled some of the glaring gaps in the record, especially from the 1930s through to the 1960s. Observations which pepper the systematic list have therefore

24

been drawn from his books and articles. This in no way reflects his immense contribution to ornithology, or for that matter to the island of Skye, not just for those of us fortunate to live here, but for the many climbers and naturalists who have found his writing inspirational.

Individuals who study Golden Eagles and birds of prey generally tend to be of a special breed, and few around today, will have failed to be motivated by Seton Gordon's *Days with the Golden Eagle*, a classic of its type, recently re-published. The history of persecution of birds of prey in Scotland is a sad reflection on those privileged minorities who have had the responsibility to own and manage wild land. Seton Gordon moved easily in 'landed' circles as well as amongst gamekeepers, and was not shy to express his opposition to those involved. He lived to see Ospreys return to breed in his beloved Speyside. How much he would have enjoyed watching Red Kites on the Black Isle. Had he lived a little longer he might have watched White-tailed Eagles drifting along the cliffs at Rubha Hunish – that would have been something worth writing about.

The Misses Baxter and Rintoul were contemporaries of Seton Gordon and when they published the *The Birds of Scotland* in 1953, it was obvious they had been in correspondence with him and doubtless trawled his memory. It was obvious they also drew heavily on the earlier work of Gray, Macpherson and Harvie-Brown. It certainly appeared that they visited the island on several occasions and made personal observations during field trips. Baxter and Rintoul present their findings in a chronological sequence which had been adapted from the 'British List' at the time. They review the distribution of each species throughout the various areas of Scotland and in this regard treated the islands separately, Skye being one of these areas. This built on earlier work which they had published on *The Geographical Distribution and Status of Birds in Scotland* in 1928 where Skye was treated as a distinct area within the North West Highlands faunal region. When *The Birds of Scotland* was published it put the flesh on this earlier work, and has been an extremely important reference text ever since.

During the 1950s there were two other important publications both of which appeared in *The Glasgow and West of Scotland Bird Bulletin*. Iain Murray was the Headmaster of Portree High School and produced a paper on *The Birds of Skye* based on his observations, mainly in the Portree district, between 1935 and 1954. Murray appeared to be an accomplished observer and many of his records are important indicators during a period which was extremely barren in terms of recording on the island. He recorded a total of 129 species including the first proved breeding of Red-throated Diver, the first record of Blackcap, as well as interesting notes on Black Grouse and Chough. In contrast, Mr N. Henson spent only a month in Pabay during February/March 1956 but recorded several species of note including Black-tailed Godwit, Grey Plover and Knot. However, his record of a Sedge Warbler on 7 March is unusual to say the least!

The period between 1960 and the early 1990s was, in the context of Skye ornithology, extremely active and important. It covered a period of three intensive *Atlas* surveys co-ordinated by the British Trust for Ornithology (BTO). Like the rest of the country, Skye was divided up into 10 kilometre squares each of which was allocated to an individual observer, who would make a number of visits to the area and systematically record all the species found. The first *Breeding Atlas* was between 1968-72. There was then a similar survey for wintering birds, the *Winter Atlas* between 1981-84, and finally the *New Breeding Atlas* between 1988-1991. Throughout this period there was an active group of birdwatchers on Skye, but, in addition, observers came in from other areas to ensure comprehensive coverage of what were extremely resource intensive surveys. As in all surveys of this nature, there are limiting factors, including the quality of observer cover, but these were ground breaking projects, extremely important for conservation. Andrew Currie arrived in Skye as an Area Officer for the Nature Conservancy Council (NCC) in 1976 and remained in that capacity until 1990. Andrew was central to the success of many ornithological projects on Skye and acted as the local representative of the BTO. Andrew was also instrumental in getting NCC support for a winter survey of the coast of Skye and Wester Ross in 1978/79. This work by Peter Ellis, though unpublished, was highly significant in terms of the winter distribution of divers, grebes, wildfowl and waders round our coasts, and some comparative analysis with current data is being carried out by the author (McMillan in prep). Andrew was also a co-author of *The Birds of the Inner Hebrides* in the Proceedings of the Royal Society of Edinburgh in 1983, which included a systematic list of the status of land birds. Other active observers at the time included the Dix family from Kensaleyre who explored throughout the island and kept detailed records over a 20-year period. Ted Gerrard lived on Pabay between 1969 and 1980, and as far as can be established, has been the only active bird ringer to reside in Skye. During the period Ted ringed in the order of 8,000 birds on Pabay, mostly Meadow Pipits, Skylarks, Rock Pipits and Twite, species rarely caught elsewhere. His most unusual capture was three Barred Warblers on separate days in late August 1971.

Despite mushrooming interest in ornithology during the last 25 years, active recording in Skye seems to have hit a bit of a lull. Many birders would no doubt whizz through Skye en route to 'twitch' rarities on the Western Isles, but few seemed to pick up much on route. Andrew Currie continued to stimulate interest in birds in his regular column in the *West Highland Free Press*. However, few records were being sent for inclusion in the now well-established *Highland Bird Report*. Ken Crane and Kate Nellist continued their intensive study on the Golden Eagle population, some of the results of which were published in *Island Eagles* in 1999. The RSPB have had an office on the island since 1996 and most of their efforts have concentrated on monitoring the expanding White-tailed Eagle population and halting the decline in breeding Corncrakes through the development of grassland management schemes. In the last five years the author has become involved in a number of studies, including breeding Hen Harriers and Merlins, regular WeBS counts in the greater Broadford Bay, and surveys of wintering divers. Roger and Pat Cottis have co-ordinated breeding Heron and other BTO surveys, as well as recording extensively in the Sleat area.

Scanning for Divers in Sleat © skye-birds.com

David Rogers, Alan and Elaine Horner and Martin Benson have regularly checked and counted areas around the greater Broadford Bay area, which has highlighted many interesting passage movements of waders and wildfowl. In the Glendale and Dunvegan areas, Geoff Lawson and Andrew Stables have observed some unusual vagrants which might indicate that the unexpected can occur on the island in favourable conditions, at the proper locations. The author launched a dedicated web site in 2004 – skye-birds.com – and this is helping to stimulate interest and recording and the increasing number of records suggest this is achieving its objective. The challenge now is to build on all of these contemporary records, to help fill the gaps, and to encourage others to go out and look. There is no shortage of potential sites of interest and the following chapter explores only a few.

4. WHERE TO FIND BIRDS ON SKYE

With a land mass covering 535 square miles, at no point more than 5 miles from the sea, fiordic lochs penetrating deep inland towards a huge and spectacular mountain mass, Skye allows you to experience a whole range of species from pelagic to upland montane, at virtually the same time. It is quite possible to sit with Golden Eagles and Ptarmigan in the Cuillin and, with a good telescope, watch rafts of Manx Shearwaters on Loch Scavaig below. It is equally possible to see Golden or White-tailed Eagles from virtually any public road in Skye, or for that matter from the Co-op car park in either Broadford or Portree. The scattered crofting communities of Skye are host to a wide range of species and the townships around Staffin, Dunvegan, Broadford and Kyleakin, as well as Portree itself, provide shelter from the vagaries of the weather and additional feeding opportunities.

The author lives in the small crofting and fishing village of Elgol where his wild garden of over an acre regularly hosts over 50 Twite, as well as frequent appearances by Wheatear, Stonechat, Raven, Merlin, the occasional White-tailed Eagle and even an overflying Red-throated Diver. The simple message from this is that it is well worth looking for birds **anywhere** on the island. Like most things in life, the greater the effort, the better the rewards, and as most species are under-recorded, and many areas totally unwatched, observations could be extremely valuable for future conservation.

Over the last few years, the following sites, shown on the map overleaf, have been regularly watched. All can be viewed easily, and there are no access difficulties. Many are part of coastal or other walks, which allow the best of birding in spectacular scenery. Don't expect to see huge numbers of birds because by and large the habitats are not extensive or particularly species rich, but should provide quality rather than quantity. During the breeding season all birds are susceptible to disturbance, not just the rarer species, so please avoid disturbing birds at this sensitive time. Regardless of the season, make sure you are properly equipped for all weathers, as conditions on Skye can deteriorate rapidly. As many of the sites are coastal, a good pair of binoculars is essential and a telescope an advantage.

Broadford Bay

This is probably the best bird watching spot on Skye. It provides feeding opportunities for waders and wildfowl. Geographically it is ideal, as birds are funnelled into the area on migration, particularly from the north. It is also well sheltered from the prevailing south-westerlies. Although the Bay itself can look pretty empty at times, there are nooks and crannies such as Ardnish, Ashaig and Camas na Sgianadin which are well worth exploring, and which are all part of the wider bay ecosystem.

The area lies to the north of the A87(T) public road, the main through-way from the Skye Bridge to Portree. There are a number of areas which make good observation points:

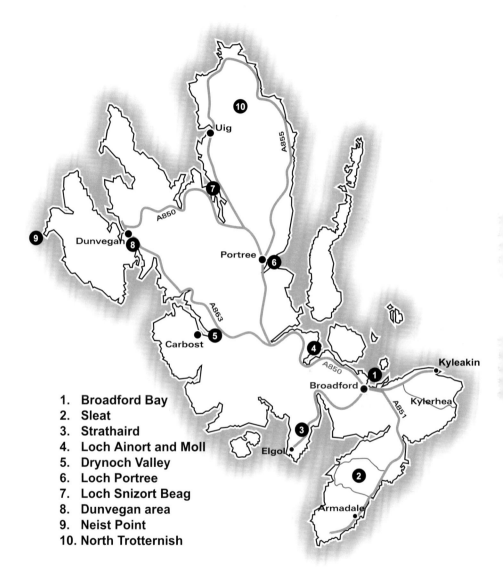

1. **Broadford Bay**
2. **Sleat**
3. **Strathaird**
4. **Loch Ainort and Moll**
5. **Drynoch Valley**
6. **Loch Portree**
7. **Loch Snizort Beag**
8. **Dunvegan area**
9. **Neist Point**
10. **North Trotternish**

1. Camas na Sgianadin (NG625255) is easily observed from the large roadside lay-by or from the forest walk which starts beside the cemetery.

2. Broadford Bay (NG650250) can be watched from numerous points including the new and old pier, and the Co-op car park. The east end is best for waders and wildfowl, especially at Harrapool and Waterloo, and birds roost on Glas Eilean. The area in front of the Hebridean Hotel Car Park provides rich feeding for passage waders and an opportunity to get close and use the car as a hide.

3. Ardnish (NG670240) is best accessed from the end of the Waterloo road at NG665240 or from Lower Breakish (NG672235) – please note there is limited parking at either. The walk round Ardnish is always worthwhile and provides a number of excellent vantage points. The islands at the east end of Ardnish are the main roosts for waders and gulls.

4. Ashaig (NG688244) is a delightful spot and easily accessed with ample parking near the cemetery. At low tide it is possible to wade across to Ardnish. There is an excellent coastal walk eastwards to Lusa where sea watching is possible from various observation points.

Broadford Bay from Ardnish © skye-birds.com

The site has potential all year round. Though the intertidal zone is not extensive, it probably provides some of the richest feeding grounds along the north-west seaboard hence is a favoured stopover point during spring and autumn migration. Though there are seldom large concentrations of birds, the turnover can be significant, so regular watching will bring its rewards. Again, because of the location, birds travelling south are liable to be drawn into the area at any time, so the occasional vagrant is inevitable. The site is probably best from July to September but is also good in winter.

Waders include Black-tailed and Bar-tailed Godwits, Sanderling, Knot, Grey Plover, Greenshank, Turnstone, Purple Sandpiper and Whimbrel. Wildfowl records include Scaup, Pintail, Long-tailed Duck, Common and Velvet Scoter, Greenland White-fronted and Brent Geese. There is a small wintering population of Slavonian Grebes and it is often possible to see all three diver species, with up to 40 Great Northern Divers. There are often huge numbers of Guillemots, Razorbills and Kittiwakes offshore. Little Auks are regular in winter off Lusa. A wandering Sea Eagle will occasionally spice things up!

Sleat

Sleat, the long peninsula which stretches from Kinloch to Armadale, and eventually on to the Point of Sleat, enjoys a relatively sheltered position which contributes to its reputation as the 'garden of Skye'. It contains a number of remnant woodlands of oak, ash, hazel and birch, as well as formal mature gardens and scatterings of exotics at Armadale Castle and other locations along its eastern edge, adjacent to the A851. You will find species of woodland birds here which are difficult to spot in other parts of the island, and the richer density of species probably reflects the available shelter and cover. There are public footpaths through a number of these woodlands. Some of the native remnants are more challenging, but nonetheless are well worthy of exploration.

The coastal fringes provide only limited habitat in the intertidal zone, Loch na Dal being a good example. Offshore watching will always be rewarding and the Point of Sleat is an excellent spot for sea watching and local migration. Suggested locations, seasons and highlights are as follows:

1. Kinloch (NG700166). From the car park access can be gained to Forest Enterprise woodlands, and an enjoyable walk to the deserted village of Leitir Fura. The area contains some mature hardwood stands and much of the modern afforestation will eventually be replaced by hardwoods as part of a larger forest project. This area is probably at its best from spring through to autumn. This is a good area to look for warblers and Spotted Flycatchers in summer. It is one of the few areas on Skye where there are resident Great Spotted Woodpeckers. There is always a chance of seeing eagles, Merlins or the occasional Peregrine. Nearby Loch na Dal is always worth a scan for divers, waders and wildfowl, particularly Teal and Mergansers.

2. Armadale Castle (NG640047). Though full of exotic tree species, the policies provide an excellent sheltered garden, good for warblers and other passerines in spring and summer. A number of species, scarce elsewhere on the island, are likely to be found, including Chiffchaff, Blackcap, Garden and Wood Warbler.

3. Tarskavaig – Ord loop road (start at either NG650062 or NG673104). This unclassified road is a spectacular drive, cycle, or even a walk in itself, with classic views of the Cuillin. It is an interesting area at any time of the year. In winter some of the lochs hold Whooper Swans,

and the bays at Tarskavaig, Tokavaig and Ord are good for Great Northern Divers, Red-breasted Merganser, as well as Turnstone and the occasional Purple Sandpiper. In summer, the remnant woods beside the road are good for warblers, flycatchers and the occasional Redstart. There is every possibility of spotting a Golden Eagle from the car, or the occasional Hen Harrier or Merlin.

4.   Point of Sleat (NM563991). It is a round trip of six miles by good track and footpath to eventually reach the lighthouse. The final section can provide an interesting loop, approaching by the beautiful sandy beach at Camas Daraich, and returning via the lovely natural harbour near Acairseid an Rubha.

This is an excellent location for sea watching from spring through to autumn with Manx Shearwaters, Skuas, Gannets, Auks and gulls high on the list. It is also an arrival and departure point for other migrants 'island hopping', including birds of prey, Wagtails, Twite and Pipits, as well as waders such as Whimbrel, especially in spring. In summer and autumn, the small patches of woodland cover around the crofts are well worth checking for migrants. This is a location which is rarely visited by birders but which could reap rich pickings for those prepared to make the effort. It is also superb for cetaceans.

Point of Sleat lighthouse with Rum in the background © skye-birds.com

Strathaird

This is the peninsula which lies between Lochs Slapin and Scavaig in the south-west of Skye and is reached by following the A881 from Broadford, through the villages of Torrin and Elgol. This is a wonderful setting and the drive through the Red and Black Cuillin is one of the most spectacular on the island. There are a variety of habitats including native woodland, estuarine, open sea, and montane. Again, it is a drive on which you might see either species of eagle from the car. The Red Hills are probably the best location on the island to see Ptarmigan. Specific locations always worth a visit are as follows:

1. Loch Cill Chriosd (NG610214). This reedy roadside loch is always worth a look at any time of year. In winter it is a good place to see Whooper Swans, Goldeneye and Tufted Duck. Reed Bunting and Little Grebe breed. Moorhen and Coot, extremely rare on Skye, formerly bred here and both have been seen again in recent years. In late summer evenings Swallows and Pied Wagtails can be seen coming to roost in the reed beds. Good numbers of Lapwing breed nearby in Suardal.

Loch Cill Chriosd and Blaven © skye-birds.com

2. Loch Slapin (NG565220). The head of the loch can be easily watched from a number of roadside vantage points. It is worth watching all year round and Greenshank, Turnstone and Ringed Plover can usually be seen. Wildfowl include Wigeon, Goosander and Red-breasted Merganser. However, in favourable conditions in late spring, Scaup, Shoveler, and Brent Geese have dropped in. It is a good area to see Black Guillemot at any time of the year. Access to the lochside is also possible further west at Kilmarie (NG565170) from where it is possible to walk westwards along a coastal path to Drinan and Glasnakille. In late summer this is a super area for Auks, Gannets and gulls. Autumn and winter bring all three species of diver with maximum counts of 20 Black-throated and 30+ Great Northern.

3. Strathaird Point (NG530114). This headland is properly known as Rubha na h-Easgainne and is accessed via an indistinct coastal path from the west end of Glasnakille or by the coastal link from Elgol. This is an area of interesting limestone cliffs, which, along with Eilean na h-Airde, have scattered breeding colonies of Shags, Black Guillemots

and increasing numbers of Fulmars. Strathaird Point is excellent for sea watching and Pomarine Skuas have been recorded in May. Arctic and Great Skuas are regular in summer and autumn when the areas hosts thousands of Shearwaters from Rum, as well as huge numbers of Auks, gulls and Kittiwakes.

4. Camasunary (NG585186). Reached via a good path which starts at the car park beside the road near Strathaird Farm (NG545173), this is a spectacular location, set in the heart of the Cuillin. During the summer there is every likelihood of seeing Merlin or Golden Eagle. Golden Plover are scarce but listen for them on Am Mam or neighbouring hills. The bay is a good spot for Turnstone and Ringed Plover as well as other waders such as Dunlin which enjoy brief stopovers. In spring and autumn Pink-footed Geese stream over the Cuillin during migration. In winter the coastal path to Elgol is excellent for viewing Great Northern and Black-throated Divers in nearby Loch Scavaig.

Loch Ainort and Moll

This sheltered sea loch (NG550280) is easily watched from various parking spots alongside the A87(T) from Ard Dorch westwards through Luib to the junction with the unclassified loop road at NG543268. Follow the unclassified road through Moll to eventually rejoin the A87(T) at Sconser Golf Course. This is an excellent route which provides a variety of vantage points for views over Loch Ainort, then out towards Scalpay and across to Raasay. Some of the best observation points are Sròn Ard a Mhullaich (NG544274), Maol Ban (NG565298) and Maol na Gainmhich (NG563316).

This site is best from late summer through until spring. Loch Ainort is sheltered from northerly winds so can provide some respite for Guillemots and Razorbills during gales.

In late summer moulting flocks of Eider and Red-breasted Merganser gather. There is a roost at the end of the loch (NG541276) which is worth checking for passage waders. In winter all three species of diver are present and counts of 30+ Great Northern Divers is not unusual. There are normally several wintering Slavonian Grebes. Common Scoter is regular. Iceland Gulls have been recorded round the fish farms.

Drynoch Valley

The River Drynoch enters Loch Harport at NG406314, creating a compact estuarine habitat with some saltmarsh. Nearby pasture is attractive to feeding wildfowl and waders. The area is well contained and can be easily watched from the nearby B8009. Follow the road to Portnalong and Fiskavaig for further views of Loch Harport and Loch Bracadale, which is especially good for divers in winter.

This site is best in autumn and winter and Greenland White-fronted, Barnacle and Greylag Geese have been recorded. This is a good location for Teal, and Goosander is also recorded frequently. Common waders are regular, and there are always reasonably sized flocks of Curlew and Oystercatcher. Moorhen, scarce on Skye, has also been recorded.

Loch Portree

The main birding interest is in Portree Loch and the nearby Harbour. Though the loch can be reached via the Varragill River from the B883 (Braes) road, to avoid disturbing birds, there are good viewing points from the A87(T), particularly at NG475415, which overlooks the main roosting areas for wildfowl, waders and gulls. There are various access points within the town of Portree which overlook the north end of the loch and the Harbour area. From near the entrance to the Cuillin Hills Hotel at NG487438 an attractive coastal footpath leads to Scorrybreac and provides an opportunity to see the entrance to the loch and look out towards the Sound of Raasay.

Loch Portree © skye-birds.com

The site is best in autumn and winter. It provides tremendous shelter especially when winds are coming from the north, and the area is always worth a look after gales.

There is a large gull roost which is always worth checking for unusual species. Iceland and Glaucous Gulls are regular in winter. In the Harbour area you are likely to find Common and Black Guillemot in winter as well as a reasonable flock of Eider Duck. In late summer and autumn Skuas are regular in the outer Loch and Little Auk has been recorded in winter. There is an extensive intertidal zone which provides feeding for good numbers of common waders such as Curlew and Oystercatcher. Greenshank and Bar-tailed Godwit are usually present in small numbers. It is a good area for wintering Wigeon and Red-breasted Merganser. If the weather is inclement the Aros Centre provides refreshments for body and soul, as well as the RSPB Sea Eagle display and CCTV link to a nest site. During the summer months take a boat trip from Portree Harbour for a close encounter with Sea Eagles.

Loch Snizort Beag

Lochs Eyre and Treaslane are included in this general site. There are good viewing points at a number of locations adjacent to the A856 road to Uig. Skerinish Quay (NG410523), Aird Point (NG400530) and Rubha nan Cudaigean (NG384545) provide excellent opportunities for viewing the loch. The car park at the Bernisdale Free Church (NG407490) is a good viewing point for the mudflats at the head of the loch.

The site is best from late summer through autumn, and winter.

This is a favoured area by Lapwing both during passage and in winter. Other common waders are present including Greenshank, Ringed Plover, Bar-tailed Godwit and Dunlin. Wigeon, Teal, Goosander and Red-breasted Merganser are recorded regularly. The outer loch is good for divers in winter, especially Red-throated. The Aird is one of the best winter locations for Reed Bunting, and Linnet is seen frequently in summer.

Dunvegan Area

Dunvegan Castle is a major draw for visitors to the area and its mature woodland policies host a good variety of breeding passerines during the summer months. Because of its location, there is the potential for migrants in late summer and autumn. The following sites in the area are recommended:

Pool Roag towards Bracadale © skye-birds.com

1. Pool Roag (NG275435). This is a small sheltered area of intertidal mudflat which can be easily scanned from the unclassified access road to Ardroag. It is a site which is worth a look at any time of the year and is the best place on the island to see Shelduck. It provides feeding for a variety of waders and in spring and summer is likely to provide a stopover point for passage birds such as Knot and Black-tailed Godwit. The surrounding croft land is tremendous for Twite in autumn.

2. Loch Dunvegan (NG250470). There are a number of sheltered bays, inlets and islands which are always worth checking for wildfowl and waders. Eider breed on the islands and there are small numbers of Shelduck. The loch holds Red-throated and Great Northern Divers in winter.

3. Loch Suardal (NG250470) is a little gem and includes the areas to the north and south of the road. To avoid disturbing the birds, use the car as a hide. Large numbers of Whooper Swans can occur on passage and a few overwinter. Over the years the loch has hosted a number of scarce wildfowl including Garganey, Gadwall and Green-winged Teal so check everything thoroughly. It is one of the few locations on Skye where Moorhen breed. Nearby Loch Corlarach is good for Goldeneye.

4. Claigan and the Coral Beaches (NG233540). The fields at Claigan often contain good flocks of Barnacle Geese which spend most of the winter on the nearby island of Isay. The walk to the Coral Beaches and Groban na Sgeire is delightful but often busy with visitors so choose your time. There is always a chance of finding Turnstone and Ringed Plover on the shoreline, as well as Great Northern Diver, Eider Duck and Black Guillemot in the sea.

Neist Point

This is the westernmost location on Skye overlooking the minches, and probably one of its best sea watching sites. There is a public car park (NG133478) at the end of the unclassified road from Glendale and Upper Milovaig. From the car park concrete steps and a path descend to the lighthouse. There are several good observation points along the route. Nearby Loch Mòr is always worth checking for waders and wildfowl. The gardens at Waterstein provide cover for passerines on passage and are worth checking.

Neist Point © skye-birds.com

There are heavy movements of Auks, Kittiwakes, Manx Shearwaters and Skuas from spring onwards but these are especially productive from late summer. Both Storm and Leach's Petrels have been recorded. Gannets feed close inshore. Great, Arctic and Pomarine Skuas are regular. Though scarcer, Sooty Shearwaters have been seen. There is also a noticeable passerine movement which includes Wheatears, Wagtails, Robins, Thrushes and Twite. Dedicated watchers will no doubt be rewarded with a few 'firsts' for Skye. It is emphasised that as this area is rarely watched, little is known of patterns of movements and hence, what is predictable.

Though primarily a sea watching hotspot, there is always a chance of spotting both Golden and White-tailed Eagle at any time.

North Trotternish

Just as the Cuillin dominates the south of Skye, so the Trotternish ridge and the Quiraing dominate the north of the island. This is a mixed landscape of spectacular escarpments and sea cliffs, with scattered crofting townships very reminiscent of the Western Isles. Corncrakes still nest in this corner of Skye. Ring Ouzels, scarce on Skye, can be found along the Trotternish ridge. The sea cliffs provide nesting ledges for a good variety of auks and gulls. Puffins nest on a few of the offshore islands. There are a number of sites which are well worth a visit:

1. Loch Mealt (NG505650). This is one of the richest freshwater lochs in Skye, located just south of Staffin. It can easily be viewed from the nearby A855. There is also a public car park located on the east side of the road with views to Kilt Rock, and a fine vista across the sea to Raasay and Wester Ross. Loch Mealt is worth checking at any time. Tufted Duck breed regularly and Pochard have bred in the past. Greylag Geese breed, and numbers build up in late summer. Several pairs of Little Grebe breed. Whooper Swans have summered in the past. Look for Goldeneye, Barnacle Geese and other wildfowl in winter.

2. Staffin Bay (NG480690). This area includes the coast north towards Flodigarry and south towards Staffin slipway. Access is easiest via the unclassified road which leads to the slip. This site is probably best between late summer and spring. There is potential for good sea watching in the area but this has been little explored. Similarly, there is the possibility of migrants in the woodlands around Quiraing Lodge and Red-breasted Flycatcher has been recorded here in the past. The Bay has good numbers of wintering Great Northern and Red-throated Divers and is always worth checking for Scoter and Long-tailed Duck. A small flock of Barnacle Geese often winters on Staffin Island.

3. Rubha Hunish (NG410768). Not for the faint hearted, the northernmost point of Skye is well worth a visit, but requires an

awkward scramble. The coastal scenery is spectacular and it is the best place in Skye to observe breeding seabirds at close range. The site can be reached by several footpaths originating at Duntulm and Kilmaluag. Access to the point is reached by a steep path which descends from a gap to the west of Meall Tuath (NG411763). As this walk features in many of the excellent walking guides to Skye it is suggested you consult one of these in the first instance. There are spectacular cliffs in the area which contain colonies of Fulmars, Kittiwakes and Shags. However, on the east side of Hunish are several small stacks and arches which afford wonderful views of breeding Shags, Kittiwakes, Guillemots and Razorbills. This is also a prime location for sea watching, with the chance of seeing passerines on the move. The cliffs are regularly patrolled by Peregrine Falcons.

Rubha Hunish with Fladda-chùain in the background © skye-birds.com

4. Uig Bay (NG390638). Best known as the ferry departure point for Tarbert and Lochmaddy, the sheltered bay is always worth checking especially in winter. There are small flocks of Eider and Red-breasted Mergansers, and the gull flock is worth picking through for white winged visitors from the north. Great Northern and Red-throated Diver winter in the outer bay. The ferry trip is a bird watching expedition in itself and has regularly provided superb sea-watching with Sooty Shearwater, Storm and Leach's Petrels, Grey Phalarope, Sabine and Ring-billed Gulls.

5. SYSTEMATIC LIST

This is the first occasion a detailed systematic list has been published for the Isle of Skye. It is readily acknowledged that there may have been a few omissions and a number of species spring to mind which it is reasonable to assume could have occurred, but records are lacking. Research into historical sources, as well as current publications has been thorough, but unusual records may have slipped through the net. The details which follow will hopefully provide some historical context, as well as set the current benchmark for species which can be found in Skye.

From a bird watching perspective much of Skye is very poorly covered, so, unlike many parts of the country, there are lots of unexplored corners, and, consequently, opportunities to find something new. Recording has been somewhat fragmented in the past and a major objective of this publication is to encourage observers to record their sightings. To assist this, a dedicated website was launched at the beginning of 2004, skye-birds.com, which is beginning to provide a focus for information on what can be seen in the area. This should help to keep everyone, locals and visitors alike, informed of what species can be seen. You are encouraged to use this website and inform others of your observations. The site links into a number of other local and national wildlife sites and will also provide information on local events, projects and research. If you have not already done so, any observations of note will be passed to the Highland 'Recorder' for possible inclusion in the annual *Highland Bird Report*, and the *Scottish Bird Report*. Details of all these publications are available on the website.

The list is presented in a species sequence which has only recently been changed, but which follows the principles adopted by the British Ornithologists' Union's Records Committee (BOURC). It is this committee which has maintained the official British List since 1883, with regard to taxonomy, sequence, and scientific names. BOURC recently altered the English names of a large number of species on the British List and, though initially controversial, this has now been accepted in Scotland. You may therefore be unfamiliar with some of these names and to avoid confusion, a number of old names are included in parenthesis.

Skye lies at the centre of Gaelic culture and tradition. Gaelic species names have therefore been included using the work of Dr Ellen I. Garvie and published by Sabhal Mor Ostaig in 1999. This is a complex and challenging field, as there are often regional Gaelic names for the same species. Some are straight translations from English names and others are unique Gaelic names in themselves. The most common usage is shown, with examples of other known names, shown in parenthesis.

A short note on status has been included, to reflect on whether a bird is resident, whether it breeds, is a winter visitor, or occurs on passage or migration. This also includes a note on its scarcity.

The UK's leading non-governmental organisations review the status of all bird species in the country and publish a document called *Birds of Conservation Concern*. Species are listed according to various criteria relating to their population status, size and relative importance. These lists are known as the Red and Amber Lists for species whose status gives cause for concern. The remaining species are on the Green List. Species which are Red and Amber Listed for 2002-2007 are shown. A variety of criteria are used for assessing the population status and this is fully explained in a document available from the BTO.

If a species has only been recorded on a few occasions, specific details are provided. Where more general data is available, this is presented in three parts. Firstly, is the **Historical** record, in general terms up to 1959; thereafter the **Middle Period** covering 1960-1994 encompassing the *Atlas* years; lastly is the **Contemporary Period** covering the ten years up to publication, when there has been some improvement in recording, and on the basis of this, some attempt will be made to assess current status. Rather than provide whole lists of records extrapolated from the available sources, some attempt has been made to summarise these and to highlight unusual records or peak counts. Although there is a comprehensive bibliography at the end of the book, to assist readers at the outset, the following list of key sources for the different periods may be helpful. These are shown in parenthesis in the text.

Historical

(Gray) – Gray, Robert, *The Birds of the West of Scotland.* (Glasgow 1871)

(Macpherson) or (Harvie-Brown) or *The Fauna* – Harvie-Brown, J. A. & MacPherson H. A., *A vertebrate Fauna of Scotland, North-West Highlands and Skye.* (Edinburgh 1904)

(B&R) – Baxter, Evelyn V. and Rintoul, Leonara Jeffrey, *The Birds of Scotland.* (Edinburgh 1953)

Middle Period (1959-1994)

The Breeding Atlas – Sharrock, J. T. R., *The Atlas of Breeding Birds in Britain and Ireland.* (Bath 1976)

(Ellis) – Ellis, P., Internal NCC Report. Unpublished (1979)

(Thom) – Thom, Valerie M., *Birds in Scotland.* (Calton 1983)

(Reed *et al.*) – Reed, T. M., Currie, A., & Love, J. A., *Birds of the Inner Hebrides.* Proceedings of the Royal Society of Edinburgh, 83B pp449-472 (1983)

The Winter Atlas – Lack, Peter, *The Atlas of Wintering Birds in Britain & Ireland.* (Bath 1986)

The New Breeding Atlas – Gibbons, Reid & Chapman, *The New Atlas of Breeding Birds in Britain & Ireland: 1988-1991.* (London 1993)

(SBR) – annual Scottish Bird Report published by the Scottish Ornithologists' Club

(HBR) – annual Highland Bird Report which commenced in 1984.

Contemporary Period (1995 onwards)

(SBR) – annual Scottish Bird Report as above.

(HBR) – annual Highland Bird Report as above (ceased publication 1999, re-commenced 2002)

(HRSG) - annual reports of the Highland Raptor Study Group.

Migration Atlas – Wernham, Chris *et al. The Migration Atlas: Movements of the Birds of Britain & Ireland.* (London 2002)

In completing the systematic list, the major authority as to whether the record was accepted in a historical context was Baxter & Rintoul, and later Valerie Thom. From the 1980s there has probably been greater scrutiny of records, and certainly in regard to the more unusual species, these would require to be accepted by the Highland Recorder, and either be included in the *Highland Bird Report* or the *Scottish Bird Report*. The Highland Recorder now has a committee which oversees these functions. In regard to rarities, certain species require to have passed the scrutiny of either the Scottish Birds Records Committee or the British Birds Records Committee. To the uninitiated, this might appear terribly bureaucratic but it is probably quite necessary. An exception to this was *Atlas* records which were subjected to only limited evaluation. Furthermore, a number of unusual records for Skye have also appeared on websites, and in Birdline Scotland summaries. That details did not subsequently appear in the *Highland Bird Report*, or for that matter in this publication, probably reflects the fact that the reports were not supported by suitable evidence and descriptions. A number of very competent observers chose not to submit records to the Recorder, but have been extremely helpful in contributing to this book. The judgements to accept the validity of these records rests entirely with the author, and a number have been included so that a fuller picture is presented. Hopefully, this attempt to set a benchmark for birding on Skye will help to provide some guidance of what is unusual or significant, but most importantly, will encourage everyone to enjoy their birds.

Apologies are made for any omissions, errors or commissions.

MUTE SWAN   *Cygnus olor*   Eala (eala bhàn)

Has bred. Scarce migrant.

There are no historical records for Skye, either for breeding birds or for casual sightings. The only possible breeding record for the island is a report in Sillar & Mehler (1973), that 'L.A.Urquhart saw a pair of Mute Swans with cygnets at Broadford in 1959', though further details are not known.

In the winter survey of 1978/79 Ellis (1979) recorded a pair in Loch Portree from October through until February and on 14.11.1979 there is a report of 3 at the same location. During the 1981-83 *Winter Atlas* there is a record of this species from a square in the Dunvegan area. Birds were also recorded in 1981 and 1982 including a bird at Loch Pooltiel with a neck collar identifying it as a bird from the Uists. According to Ogilvie (1983) 4 juveniles marked in the Outer Hebrides were reported on Skye in 1981.

These were the only documented sources for Skye which have been found. It therefore appears that as well as an absence of historical records, the birds themselves were largely absent for 25 years, until a pair were found at Isle Ornsay on 12.1.2006. There have been several reports since.

BEWICK'S SWAN   *Cygnus columbianus*   Eala bheag

Historically an extremely rare winter visitor.

Collier (1904) recorded 5 sheltering in a sea bay during stormy weather on Raasay on 9.2.1900. However, Baxter & Rintoul (1953) say there is no record for Skye. That Collier's record was not mentioned by B&R may either be an oversight on their part or they suspected he had been confused with Whoopers. The species was certainly more common in winter in the Western Isles at this time and has been recorded on most of the islands within the Inner Hebrides. Although it is surprising that Collier did not record Whoopers during his stay in Raasay, it is nonetheless quite possible that his identification of Bewick's is accurate, the first record for the area.

In Murray's notes on *The Birds of Skye* (1954) he includes a record for March 1949 but provides no location. Murray included Whoopers in his notes so was clearly aware of the distinctions between the species.

WHOOPER SWAN   *Cygnus cygnus*   Eala (eala fhiadhaich)

**Common winter visitor and passage migrant. Has summered.
Amber list species.**

There is an early report in the *New Statistical Account* Vol. XIV p.250: 'Until St. Columba's Lake (in North Skye) was drained in 1829 it was yearly frequented by large flocks of Swans which appeared on October 25th and remained 5 months.' Gray (1875) described the Whooper as an occasional visitor to Skye. Macpherson (1904) provides an account of a variety of observations during the winter months which confirms the species as a regular visitor. (It is interesting that the lochs favoured then, eg. Loch Cill Chriosd which had a family party in 1888, are still being used to-day.) Baxter & Rintoul suggested Whoopers had decreased on Skye and were not very common in winter, the drainage in 1829 being used as the basis of their judgement! It is questionable whether after 125 years such a judgement was terribly valid.

During the 1981-83 *Winter Atlas* it was found in 13 squares. A small number of Whoopers remain with us throughout the winter, e.g. in the UK census for January 1986, only 25 birds were found on Skye, similar to the number which had earlier been suggested by Ogilvie as the winter population. The majority of birds pass through and most of these are from Iceland where the breeding population has been estimated at 16,000. Over the last 40 years there have been a number of migration projects using colour rings and body markings. A number of birds observed at Loch Suardal in the winters of 1979/80 and 1998/99 were subsequently seen later that winter in Ireland. In the autumn it is not unusual to see flocks of Whoopers on the move, usually flying in a south-westerly direction, and probably heading direct to Ireland. Satellite tracking examples shown in the *Migration Atlas* (2002) provided details on 2 birds with stopovers on Skye. The first example left Iceland on 2.11, was in Lewis on 3.11, Skye on 4.11 and landed at its wintering grounds on the Solway on 5.11. A different bird on return migration left the Solway on 11.3, was on Skye the following day, left Lewis on 16.3 and arrived on Iceland on 17.3. Both these examples indicate how mobile the population is, but also suggest that large numbers of birds probably fly over Skye but are undetected. The biggest recorded count was 160 heading north through Strath Mor at the head of Loch Slapin on 8.4.2004, probably forced to fly low because of dense cloud. Other passage counts include 38 at Loch Suardal on 7.3.1977 and 75 there on 23.2.1983. A total of 59, in several groups, flew through Broadford Bay on 5.10.2001 and were obvious migrants heading south-west. Recent records suggest birds continue to move south in November.

Though small parties overwinter at a number of locations, overall winter numbers are probably below 20. Loch Suardal is the most favoured site. Though birds have not been proved to breed on Skye, there are occasionally records in summer such as a single bird near Dunvegan on 9.6.1993 and an adult at Loch Mealt, Staffin, on 25.6 and 9.8.1996. A pair summered in 2006.

PINK-FOOTED GOOSE   *Anser brachyrhynchus*

Regular passage migrant in spring and autumn.   **Amber list species.**

Although MacGillivray stated it had been shot in Skye it is surprising that Gray, *The Fauna*, and Baxter & Rintoul make no comment on the species though historically it must have overflown the island in significant numbers. However, it is mentioned by Macpherson in a note in *The Zoologist* of 1889, which had obviously been overlooked.

Sillar & Meyler quote Seton Gordon that the species 'was found on boggy land on the moors of Skye and on uninhabited islands round the coast in winter and until the first week in May.' However, there is a lack of supporting evidence for this observation, which does seem unusual. Pink-footed Geese are certainly much more common now than in historical times, but considering that most of the 200,000 population from Greenland and Iceland winters in Scotland and England, recent observations suggest there is a significant spring and autumn passage over Skye. There is no better sight nor sound than to watch Pink-footed Geese winging their way across the Cuillin heading south-east to the Perthshire farmlands, probably the first landing point on their long journey. However, current records suggest very few birds stop off on Skye, perhaps only small groups affected by bad weather, or the odd bird weakened by the journey. A group of 44 at Ardnish on 6.5.07 was unusual. Feral birds have also been recorded with Greylags.

GREATER WHITE-FRONTED GOOSE   *Anser albifrons*   Gèadh bhla

Winter visitor in small numbers.   **Amber list species.**

There are only 2 records referred to by Macpherson, 1 at Loch Eishort in 1890 and another in 1901. Collier recorded small flocks on Raasay, in early October of both 1896 and 1898. Perry refers to a flock of 50 over Scalpay.

By the 1950s a flock of c20 was wintering with regularity around Dunvegan and Loch Snizort and by 1978 this had increased to 75. By December 1978 a flock of c40 birds was also regularly wintering in the Broadford area although according to T. Gerrard (pers. comm.) a flock of 31-36 birds had been wintering on Pabay since 1969. There were reports of small flocks in 4 squares during the 1981-83 *Winter Atlas*. However it is suspected that these sightings refer only to the 2 discreet flocks which moved around to feed.

The species which winters in Skye is of the Greenland race *flavirostris* which nests solely in west Greenland on low arctic tundra. It winters in the west of Scotland and Ireland and migration involves a stopover in Iceland. The winter population of Skye is restricted to 2 small flocks, but greater numbers may occur during spring and autumn migration. During Ellis's winter survey in 1978/79 the largest numbers were recorded in the Snizort valley, with a peak of 75 in October.

The birds which wintered in the Skeabost/Drynoch area reached a max. count of 75 on 17.11.1978 (*SBR*). The area was counted with regularity by the Dix family for 20 years but by the early 1990s the flock size had reduced to between 25-30. The last count at Skeabost was 17 on 2.12.1998 and the birds have now ceased to use the area. Though a small flock is occasionally recorded in the Drynoch valley with 45 on 28.12.2000, it certainly appeared that the Skeabost/

Drynoch flock had disappeared. However, a small flock numbering around 20 birds was suspected of being in the Kilmuir area in 2004; 36 and 30 respectively were counted on 31.1 and 5.12. It is interesting to speculate that these are the former Skeabost birds, and this small flock remains in this area.

Until recently, the Broadford area was the only site where birds can be seen with any regularity, the best counts being 82 in December 2000, 50 on 2.1.2002 and 45 on 18.2.2003. On 15.3.2002 a bird of the European race *Anser albifrons* was amongst the normal Broadford flock (*HBR*). During recent winters numbers recorded in the Broadford area rarely exceed 50. Though there was a flock of 100 birds at Broadford on 30.4.2002 it is thought that these were passage birds, as were 250+ there on 5.4.2008. Passage flocks may be recorded elsewhere and 120 at Duntulm on 7.4.2000 is a further example.

According to Fox (2003) the apparent decline and disappearance of flocks is not unusual, though the big flocks in Islay and Co. Wexford in Ireland continue to thrive and increase. Fox suggests that outlying flocks in Scotland have suffered as low intensity agricultural land has become abandoned or neglected in recent years. There has been a similar problem of flock size depletion in the Uists. In 1998 Fox suggested that the Broadford flock was stable, but although good numbers are occasionally seen, there seems to be little pattern to feeding and roosting and the flock is suspected of ranging widely. These birds are extremely susceptible to disturbance, and as a species afforded special protection by the EC Birds Directive it is of concern that birds were reportedly shot in the past at Skeabost and more recently at Broadford. Whilst the flocks on Skye are small, efforts should be made by the statutory authorities to ensure that the species is properly protected.

GREYLAG GOOSE   *Anser anser*   Gèadh glas

Breeding resident. Passage migrant.   **Amber list species.**

There is evidence in *The Fauna* to suggest the species bred in Skye at the latter part of the 19th century. However, nests were often 'molested'. It was also a winter visitor in small numbers. Seton Gordon (1931) recorded that during the first week of August, Greylags appeared in the north of Skye and suggested that these were Sutherland birds which remained for several weeks. Baxter & Rintoul do not elaborate further. According to Henson there were 26 birds in the Pabay 'island' flock in 1956.

It was confirmed as breeding in 2 squares during the 1968-72 *Atlas* and there was little apparent change by 1988-91. It is surprising that during the 1981-83 *Winter Atlas* it was only recorded in one square. As well as a small resident population which is probably sedentary but increasing, there is visible migration of Icelandic Greylags in autumn and spring, most of which winter in the east of Scotland. However, it is reasonable to assume that some of these birds may stop over in Skye dependent on weather conditions.

Greylags now breed in a number of localities around the coast of Skye, though they probably still favour small offshore islands. There is also an increasing non-breeding population. In 1983 Ogilvie and Atkinson-Willes suggested that pairs breeding on Skye were descendants from introduced birds but it is not known whether that remains the position today. A census in August 2008 suggested an island population of around 500 birds which included a count of 180 in the Feorlig/Roag area on 3.8.2008. A big count of 248 between Mingay, Clett and Waternish on 3.7.2008 may have been associated with moulting birds.

CANADA GOOSE — *Branta Canadensis*

Scarce passage migrant.

The only recent records which could be traced for Skye were from Raasay on 5.6.1984, and during the 1988–91 *Breeding Atlas*, from a square in the north-west of the island. However, between 2005–08 small numbers have been recorded annually.

BARNACLE GOOSE — *Branta leucopsis* — Cathan (giùran)

Winter visitor in small numbers. Passage migrant.   **Amber list species.**

It was suggested in *The Fauna* that it is a 'winter visitant, stragglers occasionally visiting Waternish and Dunvegan Loch from the Outer Hebrides, especially in early spring.' Small flocks were occasionally recorded in winter on Raasay by Collier. Baxter & Rintoul describe it as a winter visitor to Skye but not in very large numbers, the Ascribs being a favourite haunt.

The largest flocks are located on Isay, Trodday and the Ascribs from which they will range to the main island, and also exploit nearby islets such as Staffin Island, Tulm Island and Eilean Beag. The population may also range to the Shiants and the Sound of Harris (A. Currie pers. comm.) As part of an ongoing national survey, an Aerial Census was conducted between 1957–2008 with the following results:

	Feb.1957	Mar.1961	Mar.1965	Mar.1973	Mar.1978	Apr.1983	Mar.1988	Mar.1994	Mar.2003	Mar.2008
Isay	151	140	420	297	290	220	245	370	190	316
Ascrib Isl.	193	122	308	132	140	172	100	40	74	79
Trodday	182	108	264	143	94	90	5	NC	102	56

The birds which winter in the west of Scotland and Ireland come from a population which breeds in east Greenland, and uses Iceland as a staging post during migration. Several birds ringed in Greenland in the 1950s were subsequently recovered on Skye. During the 1981-83 *Winter Atlas*, flocks were recorded from 6 squares in the north of the island. During March/April 1983 a further count on Isay revealed 250 birds.

Further counts include 80 at Staffin Island 10.12.1978 (*SBR*). During co-ordinated counts in the winter of 1978/79 Ellis recorded an island max. of c400, which is slightly below the level recorded in the aerial survey.

Other than the aerial surveys, the only recent counts of note include c200 on Isay on 26.2.2001 and an estimated 300 there on 20.3.2004. Other migrants will also pass through Skye, and 48 in 3 groups which came off the sea at Ashaig near Broadford on 27.10.2001 never landed and continued to the south-west, perhaps bound for Islay. The size of the current winter population appears to have changed little since the 1950s and as birds continue to favour offshore islands it can be difficult to monitor. A small flock of 60–80 birds is regularly recorded in the Staffin area and there are other records of small groups in the Kilmaluag area, probably the Trodday birds.

The *Highland Bird Report* of 1996 reported a single bird associating with a Black Faced x Cheviot sheep for up to 2 years, calling when other geese flew overhead. Its ultimate fate is not known. A report of 3 birds on Clett on 3.7.2008 may refer to feral birds.

BRENT GOOSE   *Branta bernicla*   Gèadh got (guirnean)

Regular passage migrant.   **Amber list species.**

Macpherson regarded it as a winter visitor, parties occasionally frequenting the Ascribs, though it had also been recorded at Waternish and Glendale. Collier had also recorded it regularly on Raasay on autumn passage. Those recorded were of the pale-breasted form (*B.b.hrota*). This was confirmed by Baxter & Rintoul who said it occurs as a passage migrant and sometimes in winter.

The sub-species which occurs on Skye is the Light-bellied Brent Goose *hrota* and those recorded here, mainly in autumn, probably originate in the eastern Canadian high arctic, and are on route to their wintering grounds in Ireland. It is suspected their route crosses the Greenland Ice Cap and they may stop off on the west coast of Iceland for 2/3 weeks before continuing their journey. It is known that most fly direct to Ireland and those which occur annually on Skye, especially in the autumn, may have been wind assisted, as a number of flocks passing over Broadford are moving in a distinct south-west direction, presumably correcting themselves and heading for Ireland. There are likely to be annual variations in the numbers seen, and in autumn most birds are recorded in September and October, and 22 on 25.8.2008 was early and unusual. Birds are occasionally seen on return spring migration, usually in May, but again this may be weather dependent, for example 24 in Loch Slapin on 2.5.2001 had certainly been blown in by a fierce westerly and poor visibility.

Thom (1986) reported that flocks of up to 150 were recorded from Skye and the records of 150 at Broadford on 30.9.1977 and 21.9.2004, and 172 on 26.9.2008 remain the max. counts. Most skeins and groups which stop to re-fuel tend to be smaller than 50 and occur regularly throughout September and October. The majority of observations are in the Broadford Bay area but a flock of 60 was recorded at Loch Ainort on 27.9.1978. On 27.9.2002 a skein of 20 flew south off Neist Point suggesting many birds may by-pass the west coast of Skye completely. Spring returners have been recorded at Loch Slapin, Ord and Isle Ornsay.

Unusually, there is only a single report of a dark-bellied bird at Glen Brittle on the exceptionally late date of 7.6.1993.

COMMON SHELDUCK   *Tadorna tadorna*   Crà-ghèadh

Breeding resident in small numbers. Passage migrant. Amber list species.

It was described by Gray as numerous on Skye, a status not confirmed by Macpherson, who found it rather scarce. Macpherson did confirm a number of breeding reports, especially from islands such as Isay, where presumably it could nest in peace. Though it had occurred on Raasay it did not breed according to Collier. It was only found in small numbers by Baxter & Rintoul.

Shelduck normally disappear from Skye from late summer until the beginning of December when they undertake a moult migration in the Helgoland Bight of the Wadden Sea.

Breeding was confirmed in 6 squares during the 1968-72 *Atlas* and it was found in 2 additional squares in 1988-91. During the 1981-83 *Winter Atlas* it was recorded in 7 squares.

Shelduck are thinly distributed on Skye and it is difficult to make any assessment on the size of the breeding population. Distribution is clearly governed by the availability of mud or sand-flats which the species exploits for feeding. Counts of up to 30 birds have been recorded at Pool Roag near Dunvegan. Broadford Bay is another favoured site.

EURASIAN WIGEON   *Anas penelope*   Lochlannach (glas-lach)

Winter visitor in small numbers. Has bred.   **Amber list species.**

Mainly regarded by Macpherson as a winter visitor 'but in comparatively scanty numbers', the only breeding record being of pinioned birds at Waterstein. It was recorded on Raasay in winter by Collier.

It appears that the first breeding record was confirmed during the 1968-72 *Atlas*, although Thom suggested that breeding had occurred on Skye since 1950. There appears to be little evidence of breeding since, though the species is reasonably common on the coast in winter. The best winter count obtained

49

by Ellis was 91 between Broadford and Kyleakin in December, 1978. During the 1981-83 *Winter Atlas* of it was recorded from 10 squares.

Small flocks of Wigeon can be found around Skye from late August – March. The total wintering population is probably no greater than 200-300 birds and the best counts are likely to be obtained in Portree Bay and the greater Broadford Bay area. Max. counts include 69 on Loch Suardal in January, 1982, 111 at Portree Bay on 19.11.2007 and 46 at Loch Slapin on 17.10.2002. Though supposition, it is likely that this wintering population is from Iceland.

AMERICAN WIGEON   *Anas americana*

Scarce vagrant.

A male at Loch Leathan on 11-12.5.1998 was accepted by BBRC as a hybrid American Wigeon/Eurasian Wigeon.

GADWALL   *Anas strepera*   Lach-ghlas

Scarce passage migrant. Has bred. Winter visitor.   Amber list species.

Thom refers to a female Gadwall with two well-grown young at Breakish in September, 1968, which was the only record which could be traced for this species until Martin Benson found a pair on Loch Suardal on 25.10.2004. In autumn 2005 there were further records from Loch Suardal and Tokavaig. Since winter 2005/06 up to two pairs have wintered at Loch Sligachan.

EURASIAN TEAL   *Anas crecca*   Crannlach (siolta)

Scarce breeder. Winter visitor in small numbers.   Amber list species.

The Teal is mentioned for Skye in both the *Old* and *New Statistical Account* and Gray had met with it on some of the lochs. Though *The Fauna* suggested two breeding sites the species was mainly regarded as a winter visitor. Collier had found it breeding on Raasay. Baxter & Rintoul quote Seton Gordon as saying that it breeds on Skye but is not common.

During the 1968-72 *Atlas* there was confirmed breeding from 4 squares, and though the distribution had changed, similar numbers were recorded in 1988-91, confirming its breeding status, albeit in small numbers. During the 1981-83 *Winter Atlas* it was found in small numbers in 7 squares. The winter population for Skye is quite small, estimated at 100-150, and the most favoured spots are all coastal, Loch na Dal, Loch Harport, Broadford Bay and Loch Snizort Beag. In December 1978 Ellis had a peak count of 60 in Lochs Dunvegan and Pooltiel but recent counts at Broadford Bay are lower than this. The origin of these wintering birds is not known.

Teal continue to breed on small inland lochs in Skye, including a number in the middle of forest plantations, but the size of the population is not known.

GREEN-WINGED TEAL   *Anas carolinensis*

Scarce North American vagrant.

This species is recorded annually in Scotland but the only report for Skye is a record from Loch Suardal, Dunvegan, on 15.11.2000.

MALLARD   *Anas platyrhynchos*   Lach riabhach (lach)

Breeding resident in small numbers. Passage migrant.

Macpherson regarded it as resident and breeding and had found a number of nests at various places on the island. It also bred on Raasay. In May 1930 Baxter & Rintoul found the species common on Skye and also suggested that the earliest record for the island was from 1795.

During the 1968-72 *Atlas* it was obviously breeding in suitable habitat throughout the island and there was little change in status by 1988-91. Widely distributed in winter but in small numbers, it was found in most squares during the 1981-83 *Winter Atlas*. According to Ellis the overall winter population reached a peak of c350 in Jan/Feb 1979, but in scattered small flocks.

There is no evidence to suggest any recent change in status of the Mallard either as a breeding bird or in winter. A count of 142 at a Sleat Loch on 18.11.2006 was exceptional.

NORTHERN PINTAIL   *Anas acuta*   Lach stiùireach

Historical breeding record. Scarce passage migrant.   Amber list species.

The only account provided by Macpherson was of a pair at a remote hill loch near Dunvegan on 15.4.1889, whose behaviour suggested they were holding territory. The male was still holding territory on 13th May and it was later suggested there had been a nest but it had been robbed. This record must be put into context, in so far as the first breeding record for this species in Scotland was only 20 years earlier. Macpherson's record was the second and it was unfortunate its significance had not been appreciated.

It was recorded in a single square during the 1981-83 *Winter Atlas* and a pair were recorded at Loch Dunvegan on 13.2.1984, the same year in which a single bird was recorded at Loch Suardal. Some 500 pairs are thought to breed in Iceland, and 26 off Lusa on 5.10.2002 may well have been migrants heading south from that population. It is suspected that 2 pairs at Isle Ornsay on 24.4.2001 may well have been migrants returning north.

GARGANEY   *Anas querquedula*   Lach-crann

Scarce passage migrant.   **Amber list species.**

Baxter & Rintoul record 4 males and 3 females at Loch Suardal, Dunvegan, on 28.3.1943, which remains the only record for the island.

NORTHERN SHOVELER   *Anas clypeata*   Gob-leathann

Rare passage migrant.   **Amber list species.**

Macpherson suggests in *The Fauna* that the first authenticated record for Skye was a male shot at Claigan, Dunvegan, on 29.3.1892. Collier also had a bird on Raasay in February, 1904.

There were no records during the *Atlas* years, though there is a report of 2 at the Storr Lochs on 15.12.1986. However, there are records of a number of passage birds during the last few years. A pair was at Loch Suardal, Dunvegan, on 23.4.1997. There were 3 at Loch Slapin on 2.5.2001 which followed a period of westerlies with poor visibility. At Waterloo, Broadford, there was a female on 4.11.2002 and a male on 20.3.2003. There was a pair on Loch Portree on 25.4.2004, and a drake at Ardnish on 13.4.2007. It is thought that some of these birds may have been Icelandic migrants.

COMMON POCHARD   *Aythya ferina*   Lach mhàsach (lach/tunnag)

Has bred. Rare passage migrant.   **Amber list species.**

According to Macpherson the species occurred occasionally on passage and he recorded a small flock of 16 males at Loch Mór near Neist Point on 7.12.1892. Interestingly, when disturbed the flock flew west over the Minch. Collier had also recorded it on Raasay.

There is confirmed breeding, the first and possibly only record for Skye, in the 1968-72 *Atlas*. During the 1981-83 *Winter Atlas* it was recorded in 4 squares, all in the north of the island.

An analysis of records of this species suggests it was seen regularly in small numbers during the 1970s and 1980s from October to April but appears to have declined since. The most favoured locations were in the north of the island at Loch Mór and Loch Mealt. There were 7 at Loch Mór on 12.12.1977 and the only recent record was 5 at Loch Greshornish on 12.11.2007.

TUFTED DUCK   *Aythya fuligula*   Curracag (lach sgumanach)

Rare breeding resident. Passage migrant.

Though there is reference to this species in *The Fauna* the record referred to is a little vague. However in an earlier note in *The Zoologist*, Macpherson reported that several had visited a pool in Waternish late in 1882, and that one had been shot. The Tufted Duck certainly appears to have been extremely rare in the north of Scotland at the end of the 19th century though at that time it was thought to be expanding its range. Such a distinctive duck would have been difficult to overlook. Collier, however, stated it was not uncommon on Raasay in winter. According to Berry (1939) a pair bred on Skye in 1929. When Baxter & Rintoul visited Skye in 1930 they found a pair on Loch Cill Chriosd on 21.5. Though they thought they were nesting a subsequent visit proved negative.

This species favours the richer feeding lochs located in the north of the island. Breeding records were confirmed during the 1968-72 Atlas when it appears to have bred in 4 squares. However, this had declined to one square by 1988-91. In the inter-Atlas years however, there was a report of 20 pairs at Loch Mealt in July, 1984. Thom reported that it bred sporadically on Skye. During the 1981-83 *Winter Atlas* it was recorded in 8 squares. What is significant however, is the apparent size of the flocks. In 2 squares, flocks in excess of 25 birds were recorded, which in itself would be unusual for Skye. Exceptionally however, a flock of more than 95 birds was recorded in another square.

There is little evidence that the status of the Tufted Duck has changed. Loch Mealt remains its favourite loch with a brood of 5 there on 9.8.1996 and a count of 15 on 12.4.2002. There are scattered records from elsewhere. Small flocks are also recorded on passage.

GREATER SCAUP   *Aythya marila*   Lach-mhara

Regular passage migrant. Has wintered.   **Amber list species.**

Macpherson provides accounts of a number of birds, invariably shot over the winter months but there is no suggestion that the species was a regular visitor to Skye. Collier recorded a small group during the winter of 1897/98 and said they were also occasionally seen off the coast of Raasay.

There is a record of a female at Loch Ainort on 11.2.1979. During the winter survey of 1978/79 Ellis recorded 3 at Broadford in October and singles elsewhere. During the 1980s it was often recorded in winter, usually singles, although there were 2 at Loch Suardal on 27.4.1987. More recently, the best records have been 32 off Waterloo, Broadford, on 10.10.1998 (7 males and 25 females), and 60 at Broadford Bay on 24.9.2004, with smaller numbers regularly each autumn. Birds were also recorded at Loch Mealt in September, 2001. These passage records are probably not surprising as, according to the *Migration Atlas*, the wintering population in Britain and Ireland is mainly Icelandic in origin. Records for Skye, mainly in autumn but also in spring, are likely to involve these birds. A pair at Loch Slapin on 2.5.2001 followed westerlies with poor visibility and were likely to have been returning Icelandic birds.

COMMON EIDER *Somateria mollissima* Lach lochlannach (lach mhòr)

Common breeding resident. **Amber list species.**

The *Old Statistical Account* (1795) suggested that Eiders nested on the islands in Uig Bay. However, the next subsequent record was 1884 when 3 pairs nested on the Ascribs (Macpherson). Prior to this it seems to have been largely confined to the Outer Hebrides and was only present on Skye as a winter visitor. The species considerably expanded its range in the west of Scotland during the late 19th and early 20th centuries, which is well documented in *The Fauna*. Collier found them breeding in Raasay in 1897 and they subsequently increased on the island, an expansion later noted by Temperley. Baxter & Rintoul found them common in 1930 especially between Broadford and Portree. Several pairs had also been known to breed on South Rona before 1904, as by 1916 they were apparently nesting abundantly.

It was suggested in *SBR* that Gavin Maxwell's Eider farming experiment on Eilean Bàn, Kyleakin, had increased the population of breeding birds from 20 pairs in 1966 to 200 pairs by 1968 and 230 pairs by 1969. (For an account of this see *The White Island* by John Lister-Kaye.)

During the 1968-72 *Atlas*, its widespread distribution as a breeding bird was confirmed, being recorded in every coastal square. By the time of the 1988-91 *Atlas* there was evidence of a slight decline, but it is difficult to make an assessment in terms of numbers. During the 1981-83 *Winter Atlas* it was recorded in 11 squares with the biggest flocks from Broadford Bay east to Kyleakin. Thom suggests that most of the birds breeding in the Inner Hebrides will form local moulting flocks and this can certainly be apparent in late summer. Scattered groups are present throughout the  coast and it is difficult to assess the size of the population. As examples, however, there were counts of 167 at Sconser on 31.7.1999, 130 off Ardnish, Broadford, on 13.8.2000, and 263 between Luib and Sconser on 27.8.2001.

In winter, flocks are recorded at a number of favoured localities throughout the Skye coastline. However, the only sizeable winter flock was off Kyleakin and counts there were estimated at 500 in 1968 (*SBR*). During counts by Ellis in the winter of 1978/79 the other main wintering area was between Loch na Cairidh and Loch Sligachan with a max. of 241 in October 1978. There remained a flock at Kyleakin in winter which appears to peak in December, with 300 in 1999, 400 on 17.12.2000 and 500 on 5.12.2001. However, this flock has now significantly reduced.

A great deal of data has been collected by A. Currie and others, especially during the period 1960-1990. There is now evidence to suggest a significant decline in the status of the Eider on Skye, especially in winter.

LONG-TAILED DUCK   *Clangula hyemalis*   Eun buchainn (eun-binn)

Rare winter visitor.   **Amber list species.**

It was 'met with in considerable numbers off the coasts of Skye' according to Gray. This status was not confirmed by Macpherson who had several winter records between 1887 and 1890, the largest a group of only 4 birds, so it was apparently a scarce visitor in small numbers. Collier also said it was numerous in winter, generally some distance out at sea.

Ellis had a single at Loch na Cairidh in late 1978, at which time a female was found dead at Broadford. It was recorded in a single square in the Staffin area during the 1981-83 *Winter Atlas*. A male was at Camasmore, Kilmuir, on 10.12.1986 and a pair there on 25.1.1987. Subsequently, 4 were recorded at Kyleakin on 18.10.1991, and a single male again at Camasmore on 27.12.1996.

There was a single at Waterloo, Broadford, on 16.5.2001, then 7 there between 23-25.10.2001, and 6 at Harrapool later that year. During the last few years there have been a number of records and 2/3 birds spent the winter of 2001/02 in Broadford Bay. Small numbers continue to be recorded each year. These records probably reflect increased observer coverage particularly in the Broadford Bay area, which would suggest that the species may be more regular than previously thought.

COMMON SCOTER   *Melanitta nigra*   Tunnag-dhubh (lach bheag dhubh)

Regular winter visitor and passage migrant.   **Red list species.**

There is no historical record in Gray or *The Fauna*. However, in a note in *The Zoologist* of 1886 Macpherson recorded that he had seen it twice on Skye, in May 1882 and July 1886, and that birds had been shot by a friend at Loch Bracadale. Though Baxter & Rintoul say it occurs occasionally on Skye no source is provided. However, Collier found it a regular winter visitor to Raasay.

In the 1978/1979 winter survey Ellis recorded the birds at 2 locations, a male in Glen Brittle on 8.5.1988 and 10 at Maol na Gainmich, near Sconser on 4.11.1982. There is an interesting summer report of 10 off Raasay on 27.6.95, because there is no breeding record for the area.

Since 2000 there have been an increasing number of reports reflecting increased observer coverage. A few birds may winter each year and birds have been present at Broadford Bay, Loch Slapin, Loch Ainort and Loch Eishort. Passage birds also occur and some of these may linger. For example there were 27 in Broadford Bay between 23-30.10.2001 and still 11 there on 9.11. In 2002, Broadford Bay recorded 6 on 12.5, 4 on 3.7 and 6 on 29.8. The largest count in 2003 was a group of 35 in Loch Ainort, off Luib, on 16.11. Though it is thought some of this flock dispersed, as small parties were seen at other locations in the vicinity, a core group remained until the end of the year, and 11 remained until at least 13.2.2004. On 17.1.2004 a flock of 11 was recorded near Carbost on Loch Harport and more recently the largest flock was 80 at Broadford Bay on 15.10.2007. Many of these birds are thought to be Icelandic in origin and it is significant that all the recent flocks consist almost exclusively of females and juveniles. However, there are also records in the summer months, including 30 in Broadford Bay on 6.7.2007.

VELVET SCOTER   *Melanitta fusca*   Lach-dhubh (tunnag ghleust)

Scarce winter visitor and passage migrant.   **Amber list species.**

A report of 2 off Tokavaig, Sleat, on 18.8.1969 is regarded as the first record for Skye (*SBR*). Ellis recorded a bird at Loch na Dal in December, 1978. There is a further report of a female at Staffin Slipway on 27.12.1996.

More recently there was a male off Lusa, Broadford, on 3.3.2002 which was probably the same bird recorded at nearby Ardnish on 2.4.2002. In 2004, 2 birds were recorded at Ardnish on 2.1 and one of these was still present on 25.1. A male wintered at Loch Harport between 18.10.07 and 24.4.08.

COMMON GOLDENEYE   *Bucephala clangula*   Lach chinn uaine

Common winter visitor in small numbers.   **Amber list species.**

It was regarded in *The Fauna* as a 'winter visitor, stragglers turning up occasionally' but accounts of groups of up to 14 were recorded. Collier also recorded it on Raasay.

There were 2 summer records during the 1988-91 *Atlas* but no evidence of breeding. During the 1981-83 *Winter Atlas* it was found to be well distributed, being recorded in 20 squares. The pattern in Skye is of small numbers wintering, both in sheltered sea lochs, and at suitable inland lochs. Wintering birds are likely to be from Scandinavia. Best counts include 41 at Loch na

Cairidh on 17.3.1976 (A. Currie) and 30 in the same area during Feb/March 1979 (Ellis). More recently 19 were recorded in Broadford Bay on 15.12.2001 and there is a report of 31 at Ardnish on 31.3.2002.

It is difficult to assess the size of the winter population because it is scattered between the coast and inland lochs, most of which are frost-free in winter. However, it is not significant.

SMEW *Mergallus albellus*

Extremely rare winter visitor – historical record only.

The only record which can be traced is a historical one which was not included in *The Fauna* and, probably as a result of this, was excluded from subsequent publications. In a note to *The Zoologist* in 1889 Macpherson provides a list of 'Uncommon Birds of Skye' not included in his earlier paper of 1886. Smew is listed though no detail is provided.

RED-BREASTED MERGANSER *Mergus serrator* Siolta dhearg

Breeding resident in small numbers. Common winter visitor.

Gray found it breeding on rocky islets off Skye, an occurrence confirmed by Macpherson who provided details of breeding behaviour from a variety of localities. It was also present in winter. According to Collier, it bred in great numbers on Raasay, though Temperley, in 1938, found that 'perhaps, it was breeding occasionally'. Miss Baxter found it common on Raasay in April 1939.

During the 1968-72, *Atlas* breeding was confirmed in 13 squares and was probable in 4 others. By 1988-91 there appears to have been some decline

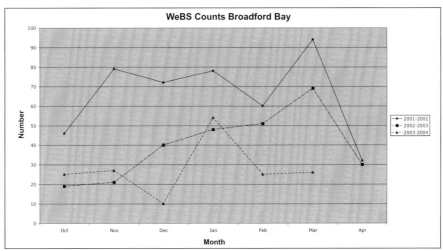

57

in distribution. The winter distribution is comprehensive, and the max. count obtained by Ellis was 91 between Loch na Cairidh and Loch Sligachan in Feb/Mar 1979. It was found in 20 squares during the 1981-83 *Winter Atlas*. Many of the wintering birds are thought to be immigrants from Iceland (Thom) and Ellis estimated a min./max. of 200-250 as the totals for Skye during the winter survey of 1978/79.

The winter totals found by Ellis are significant, and this has also been borne out during WeBS counts in the greater Broadford Bay area where there was a max. count of 94 on 3.3.2002. Broadford Bay is therefore on the threshold of being of national importance for the species, as is the coast of Skye generally. Current numbers may be greater than Ellis's estimates. One of the challenges is that birds tend to be in loose groups rather than flocks so counts can be difficult. A count of 40 on Loch Slapin on 7.12.2002 was unusual and there was a count of 43 between Luib and Moll on 17.2.2005.

From late summer a small moulting flock is present on Loch Ainort. These may be local breeding birds and the flock reached peaks of 55 on 14.10.2000, and 44 on 14.8.2005.

GOOSANDER   *Mergus merganser*   Lach/tunnag fhiacailleaach

Rare breeding resident. Occurs regularly in winter and passage.

According to Macpherson it was a winter visitant, though it seems to have been scarce. Collier found it rare on Raasay but it did occur in winter.

Sillar & Meyler report that a nest was found in June 1939, which appears to be the first confirmed breeding record. During the 1968-72 *Breeding Atlas* there were records from 5 squares. Unfortunately by 1988-91 it was only recorded in one square. It was found in 6 squares during the 1981-83 *Winter Atlas*.

It is recorded in virtually every month, usually in small numbers with a predominance of females in summer, possibly non breeders. More recently it successfully bred in the Loch Slapin area with 6 young seen on 22.6.2002. However, it is more regularly seen in late summer/autumn at locations such as Loch Ainort, Portree Loch, Loch Sligachan, and Loch Slapin as well as inland lochs. Most groups are small, numbering 4-8, so 13 at Loch Snizort Beag on 21.9.2002 was unusual, as was 18 at Loch Slapin on 16.10.2007.

RED GROUSE   *Lagopus lagopus scotica*   Coileach-fraoich (cearc-fhraoich)

Breeding resident.   **Amber list species.**

In 1773 Boswell found Red Grouse on Raasay. Many parishes list the species in both the *Old* and *New Statistical Account*. Gray regarded it as common on Skye and Macpherson stated it was 'resident and plentiful'. The species was described as fairly numerous on Raasay by Collier. However, Temperley suggested that they were now much reduced by vermin and poaching! Many estates on Skye were certainly managed for Grouse at this time and probably produced reasonable bags. When Strathaird Estate was being sold in the 1920s, the sales brochure suggested that the annual bag was 300 brace. Baxter & Rintoul said in the 1950s that 'it has now much reduced and is scarce everywhere'.

Well distributed during the 1968-72 *Atlas* with probable breeding in 19 squares and little decline by 1988-91. Recorded in 11 squares during the 1981-83 *Winter Atlas*.

Whilst suitable habitat is present throughout the island, Grouse numbers are difficult to quantify and distribution appears to be fairly sparse. Sustaining suitable heather habitat is vital for this species and overgrazing by sheep, and inappropriate muirburn, are limiting factors. The only area on the island currently managed to improve Grouse stocks is Eilean Iarmain Estate on Sleat. Here, it is not unusual to see 60-70 birds on a day's shooting and coveys of up to 8-10 birds are now being recorded. Breeding performance is very much dependent on weather conditions but numbers are generally increasing and 2003 was an exceptional breeding season. (M. Mackenzie pers. comm.)

ROCK PTARMIGAN (PTARMIGAN) *Lagopus muta* Tàrmachan (gealag bheinne)

Breeding resident.

The *Old Statistical Account* (1795) records the species from the Parish of Snizort and the *New* (1840), from Strath. MacGillivray also records them for the Cuillin and Strath mountains. Macpherson recognised in *The Fauna* that the species could be found on the higher tops, particularly the Red Cuillin; it was suggested that the hill above Sconser (Glamaig) was the best ground for Ptarmigan on Skye, a flock of 50 being seen in winter. Baxter & Rintoul say they were still nesting at Beinn na

Caillich in 1926 and Perry (1942) also found 2 pairs in the hills above Loch na Bèiste.

There was confirmed breeding from 7 squares during the 1968-72 *Atlas* but an apparent decline by 1988-91. It was recorded in only 2 squares in the Cuillin during the 1981-83 *Atlas,* and only in small numbers. Andrew Currie (in Thom 1986) suggested that the small Skye population was in decline.

Whilst the Ptarmigan is not found in the same numbers as in the historical past it can still be found in small groups in the range to the south of Kyleakin (Beinn na Caillich and Sgurr na Coinnich) as well as the Red Hills. It has recently been recorded on most of the tops in the Red Hills, the largest count being c12 on Glamaig (K. Miller pers. comm.).

BLACK GROUSE   *Tetrao tetrix*   Coileach-dubh (liathchearc)

Previously a well-established breeding resident. No recent records.
Red list species.

In both the *Old* and the *New Statistical Account* this species is listed for the Parish of Strath. In 1837 MacGillivray said it was abundant on Skye. According to Gray it was found plentifully on the Inner Hebrides, which was certainly evident as early as 1773 in Boswell's *Life of Johnson,* specifically in regard to Raasay where there were Black-cock in 'extraordinary abundance'. Macpherson suggested that that they were resident in the more wooded parts of Skye, shooting tenants accounting for birds at Drynoch in 1883, Dunvegan and Ullinish in 1889 and Waterstein in 1890. Though Collier said they were decreasing on Raasay, Baxter & Rintoul expressed the view that they remained plentiful there until about 1915. However, still on Raasay, few could be found by 1927, by 1932 they were very rare, and by Temperley's time, they were extinct! On Skye itself Baxter & Rintoul state it was quite the exception to see the species by 1927 although Perry was aware of 4 pairs above Loch na Bèiste around 1940. Murray recorded a cock shot at Skeabost in 1951, but none were recorded subsequently and he expressed the opinion that the species was probably extinct by 1954.

According to the 1968-72 *Atlas* the species was present in a single square on Raasay. Unfortunately it has not been possible to establish the detail of this, but, if genuine, it was a significant record, probably the last made of this species, certainly on Raasay. Though Thom had stated in 1986 that the species was recently extinct in Skye, Andrew Currie had records at Kylerhea around this time. However, there were no records during the 1988-91 *Atlas.* The *Highland Bird Report* includes a record from Broadford on 19.5.1988. This appears to be last 'official' record for Skye.

Though there have been several reports of birds during the last few years, these are difficult to confirm. It is perfectly possible that occasional birds might stray to the west coast but this must be put in the context of the perilous position of the population elsewhere in Scotland where prime habitat still exists. Whilst there is always the possibility of birds occurring, the chances of the species being re-established as a breeding bird on Skye are extremely remote, and there is no breeding record for over 50 years.

RED-LEGGED PARTRIDGE *Alectoris rufa*

Scarce breeding resident (introduced).

There is a record of 20 at Ord, Sleat, on 26.9.1986. It later transpired that the birds had been used in a film advertising chocolate which was being 'shot' at Kinloch House, and had sought their freedom after a starring role. Though they remained in the vicinity for 2 weeks their freedom was probably short lived, and they would no doubt be a welcome delicacy for the local predators.

Coincidentally, Sleat is now the location for an introduction for game purposes by Eilean Iarmain Estate. Since 2000, approx 200 birds have been released each year. It is felt that Red-Legged Partridges are hardier and will cope well with the vagaries of the Skye weather, a fact confirmed in 2003 when at least 2 broods of chicks were reared in the wild (M. MacKenzie pers. comm.). Birds were also released at Greshornish in 2006. However there are no recent reports from these areas.

GREY PARTRIDGE *Perdix perdix* Peurtag (cearc-thomain)

Historically a breeding resident. Recently re-introduced.
Red list species.

In the *Old Statistical Account* (1795) it bred at the parishes of Snizort and Portree. It remained a breeding bird in Gray's time and it was certainly a breeding resident in the north of Skye towards the end of the 19th century (Macpherson). At this time it was introduced on the Strathaird Estate. Collier introduced them on Raasay but apparently they did not breed and disappeared. Seton Gordon (1938) suggested it was extinct on Skye although within his memory as many as 50 brace had been got on one estate in a season. There is much evidence of the species being introduced for sporting purposes during the 20th century so it is difficult to establish what the 'natural' status of the species was.

During the 1988-91 *Atlas* the species was recorded in a square on Sleat – however details of this significant sighting are not known, or whether this resulted from a recent estate release. Eilean Iarmain Estate has now started a release programme in Sleat where 50 were released in 2003, but there are no recent reports.

COMMON QUAIL　　　*Coturnix coturnix*

Extremely rare summer visitor.

Though MacPherson made reference to this species having been recorded on Skye he provided no detail. There was an apparent absence of records until a calling bird was at Kilmuir, Trotternish in May and June 2007.

COMMON PHEASANT　　　*Phasianus colchicus*

Breeding resident.

This species would be widely distributed in the historical period when there were a number of active sporting estates. In recent years Eilean Iarmain estate has sustained a release programme and these birds are recorded widely in Sleat and as far north as Broadford. A single in Staffin on 17.11.2007 was unusual.

RED-THROATED DIVER　　*Gavia stellata*　　Learga chaol (learga uisge)

Breeding resident. Occurs on passage and in winter in small numbers. Amber list species.

According to Macpherson it was a winter visitor to Skye, although he does make reference to a former breeding site in the Waternish area. From Collier's paper on *The Birds of Raasay* he obviously had a pair on a freshwater loch on the island but, perhaps deliberately for fear of oologists, did not say whether

they bred. Baxter & Rintoul do not mention this species in the context of Skye. Although Perry recorded singles off the coast of Skye he suggested that they bred on the mainland. Murray reported that several pairs bred and this appears to be the first evidence of breeding. Kenneth Richmond (1968) quoted Seton Gordon that the numbers of the species breeding was still very small.

During the 1968–72 *Atlas* birds were present in 21 squares and breeding confirmed in 14 of these, and whilst there were some changes in distribution by 1988-91 the overall population appeared unchanged. Thom commented that there had been considerable expansion of breeding range in the first half of the 20th century and that this expansion appeared to be continuing. This extension of breeding range was certainly apparent on Skye and Neil Roberts located a good number of pairs from widespread locations. During a survey on Raasay in 1982, Church and Lodge located 5 pairs, 3 of which were successful, fledging 4 young, further clear evidence of expansion on an island which had been relatively well 'watched' up to WW2.

During Ellis's winter survey the peak monthly count was in Jan/Feb 1979 when 27 were recorded between Loch na Cairidh and Loch Sligachan. He also recorded 11 in Loch Snizort in Feb/March 1979. Peak counts by T. Dix were also in early spring with 16 off Moll on 8.2.1983 and 15 off Trotternish on 13.2.1983. During the 1981-83 *Winter Atlas* the species was recorded in 11 squares.

Following the breeding season it is suspected that most birds disperse southwards in September/October. Some have been recorded back on their breeding lochs in March and there is a notable movement of birds back up the east coast of the island in early spring –e.g. on 13.3.2002 9 were counted heading north through Loch na Cairidh, between Dunan and Scalpay. This is a location favoured by the species and recent counts there include 13 on 13.1.2004 and 18 on 21.3.2004. It is also significant that peak totals for Skye recorded by Ellis were in early spring with a total of 51 in Jan/Feb and 48 in Feb/March 1979. These counts may well have contained early returning breeders.

The best recent midwinter counts include 9 in Loch Snizort on 2.12.2003, 13 between Broadford and Sconser on 30.12.2002 and 19 between Camas na Sgianadin and Ard Dorch on 30.12.2003 and 28 between Camas na Sgianadin and Sligachan on 22.11.2006. Small numbers can be found wintering in the coastal waters of Skye, particularly on the sheltered east coast. The origins of these birds may be complex because apart from birds from further north in Scotland, e.g. Orkney and Shetland, birds from Iceland, Greenland and Scandinavia may also winter here.

During the 1980's it was estimated that up to 30 pairs may have bred in the area (N. Roberts pers. comm.). On the basis of recent information obtained from K. Crane, K. Nellist and others it is estimated that c50 pairs may breed on Skye. A national survey conducted in 2006 using randomly selected squares confirmed this apparent increase.

BLACK-THROATED DIVER   *Gavia arctica*   Learga (learga choilearach)

Has bred. Winter visitor and passage migrant.   Amber list species.

It was regarded as a 'casual visitant' by Macpherson who then recorded that Captain Cameron (of Glen Brittle) 'took a clutch of eggs of the Black-throated Diver in a loch on Soay, which he then rented, in 1882; and, in the following year, a representative of the Land League informed him that the old birds had bred there again that season (1883), but that he had boiled and eaten the eggs'. There were further breeding attempts from the Bracadale area where birds successfully reared 2 young in 1894. Although Collier had seen them on a suitable loch on Raasay, they did not breed. He also saw them offshore in winter. Baxter & Rintoul do not add to this other than to say that in May 1930 several birds were seen on the sea lochs.

During the 1968-72 *Atlas*, breeding was confirmed on three sites. Thom suggested that the species colonised a number of the Inner Hebrides islands in the first half of the 20th century but also added that there had been no recent breeding record from Skye. There is an unconfirmed report of a pair with 2 young at a site in 1987. Although birds were present in 3 squares during the 1988-91 *Atlas* there was no evidence of breeding.

In so far as winter totals are concerned, 15 were recorded in Loch Ainort in April, 1976. In the 1978/79 winter survey conducted by Ellis, peak counts of 20 occurred in the area between Braes and Loch Portree. A single count of 25 was recorded in Portree Bay in February, 1982. During the 1981-83 *Winter Atlas* it was recorded in 8 squares. During the 1984/85 winter survey of coastal birds (Moser *et al.* 1987) a total of 26 birds were found on the coastline of Skye and the small isles.

There is no recent breeding data. There is however, continued evidence of wintering birds on the coast of Skye with birds recorded from August through to April. Donald (2000) provided details of post breeding congregations in the sea off Wester Ross at Gairloch and Applecross. It may be that this population, assumed to be a significant part of the small Scottish breeding population, also disperses along the nearby Skye coast.

More recently, birds have been found off the west coast of Skye with max. counts of 16 at Loch Scavaig on 17.10.1999 and 19 in Loch Slapin on 12.3.2002. Counts in late 2003 suggest that there is a wintering population of 20-30 birds between Lochs Scavaig and Slapin with a min. of 26 on 8.12. There were 26 off Kilmarie, Loch Slapin, on 21.4.2005, and 28 there on 25.3.2006. Some of these birds remain late and there were still 9 on 12.5.2001 and 28.4.2003, which would suggest that some may be non breeders. On 17.1.2004 a small group of 5 were recorded in Loch Bracadale suggesting there may be other localities in Skye where the species winters, but are as yet undiscovered. As there are only thought to be around 150 summering pairs of Black-throated Divers in Scotland, the coast of Skye is an important wintering area for perhaps 20% of the Scottish population.

GREAT NORTHERN DIVER *Gavia immer* Muir-bhuachaill (bunna-bhuachaill)

Common winter visitor and passage migrant. **Amber list species.**

Macpherson stated it was a winter visitor 'haunting the Waternish Islands in December and lingering into spring, frequenting our coasts and islands, always singly, from year to year'. Collier found it common on Raasay in winter, May 15th being the latest date of their departure. Perry suggested passage in May through the Kyle at Lochalsh – 'day after day divers travelled up the Kyle. I was astonished at the numbers of them.' Murray stated they were very common offshore in winter.

The peak counts obtained by Ellis during the winter survey of 1978/79 were 38 in Jan/Feb between Kyleakin and Broadford, and 39 the following month between Loch na Cairidh and Sligachan. Ellis's peak of 145 for the Skye coast was in Feb/March 1979. During the 1981-83 *Winter Atlas* the species was recorded in 16 squares, the largest concentrations being in the east of the island. This was followed in 1984/85 by Moser's winter survey of coastal birds, which found a total of 63 birds along the areas surveyed within Skye and the small isles, a distribution of .73 per 10km of shoreline. Though this was an extremely resource intensive survey, Ellis's earlier findings would suggest that there was a significant undercount during the 1984/85 survey. Work by the author since 1999 would certainly indicate that numbers significantly higher than those recorded by Ellis winter on Skye.

There is no evidence that this species has bred on Skye though birds are recorded regularly in summer. It is a winter visitor in significant numbers which starts to arrive in early October and stragglers are still present in early June. It therefore spends more time in the west coast of Scotland than it does in its breeding grounds of Iceland, Greenland and Arctic Canada. It can be found throughout the coast of Skye and its offshore islands but the biggest concentrations are normally found in the sheltered bays of the east coast and in the south of the island. Lochs Scavaig, Slapin, Eishort and the Sound of

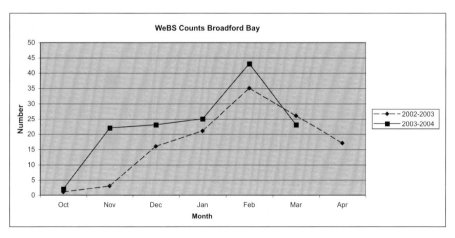

Sleat are important as is the coast from the Skye Bridge through Broadford Bay, outer Lochs Ainort and Sligachan and the sound between Raasay and Scalpay. Peak counts include 26 in Staffin Bay on 1.2.1984, 21 in Loch Slapin on 23.4.2000, 25 in Broadford Bay on 14.4.2002, 30 between Luib and Sconser on 13.3.2002, 35 in Broadford Bay on 9.2.2003 and 26 there on 23.3.2003, 36 on Lochs Eishort/Slapin on 6.11.2003, and 40 between Camastianavaig and Ard Dorch on 3.12.2003. The Loch Bracadale area is also important and there was a count of 30 on 17.1.2004. Broadford Bay has been counted systematically as part of WeBS counts during the last 2 winters and the results are shown below. Numbers tend to peak in February which is thought to reflect a build up of spring birds moving north prior to dispersal to breeding areas.

Thom estimated that 1000-1500 winter off the Scottish coast. Given the numbers now found in Orkney, Shetland, and the Western Isles this figure is a significant under-estimate. This is a species which is difficult to census as it is an adaptable feeder which can fish well offshore. On Skye, birds tend to feed singly during daytime and at dusk they move together towards overnight roosts in deeper water. Several roosts have now been located and counting birds heading to roosts is probably the most accurate method of assessing the population size. This method was adopted by the author in early 2004 resulting in counts of 44 birds in Loch Slapin on 19.2 and 42 birds between Broadford and the Skye Bridge on 23.2, 39 birds on Loch Eishort between Ord and Achnacloich on 8.3. and 60 between Ardnish and the Skye Bridge on 9.3. There were 59 in Loch Slapin on 25.3.2005, 42 on 14.3.2006 and 39 on 21.2.2007. It is therefore suspected that the wintering population of Skye is between 300-400 birds, and this may increase in spring, underscoring the importance of the Skye coastline for this well travelled visitor.

YELLOW-BILLED DIVER (WHITE-BILLED DIVER)   *Gavia adamsii*

Scarce winter visitor.

A single at Loch Ainort on 14.4.1976 was the first record for Skye. There were further records in 1983 with a first-year at Fiscavaig on 19.5 and an adult at Uig Bay between 23-25.5. There was a report from the Aird of Sleat on 9.11.2002 but it is not known whether this record was accepted.

LITTLE GREBE   *Tachybactus ruficollis*   Spàg-ri-tòn (fàd-monadh)

Breeding resident, mainly offshore in winter.

'Well known' on Skye according to Gray. Macpherson gave no evidence of breeding suggesting it was a winter visitor, as many as 5 or 6 being seen together in the shelter of the Skinidin islands. Before 1904 Collier had found it breeding on Raasay and this was later confirmed by Temperley. B&R found 2 pairs with young on Loch Cill Chriosd in 1930. Murray found the species common on the sea in winter and a few pairs bred on the Storr Lochs.

During the 1968-72 *Atlas* there were records from 12 squares and confirmed breeding in 7 of these. However, by 1988-91 there appeared to have been a decline with birds apparently absent from 7 sites formerly occupied.

Recorded from 9, mostly coastal, squares during the 1981-83 *Winter Atlas*.

Best counts include a max. of 8 on Lochs Fada and Leathan on 20.4.1976 and a count of 12 on Loch Mealt on 18.9.1986. In 2003 an adult was still feeding a well grown young on Loch Mealt on 1.10.

Little Grebe breed on freshwater lochs in Skye and tend to move to sheltered coasts in the winter. In mild winters some may remain on their breeding lochs.

GREAT CRESTED GREBE   *Podiceps cristatus*   Lapairin (lachair)

Scarce autumn and winter visitor.

There is a report in the *HBR* from Ardnish, Broadford, on 2.1.2002. There is also an unconfirmed report from near Staffin in September 2003.

Though scarce on the west coast, it is highly likely that wandering birds will occasionally occur on Skye.

RED-NECKED GREBE   *Podiceps grisegena*

Scarce autumn and winter visitor.   **Amber list species.**

According to Macpherson a bird in winter plumage was shot on the coast of Skye by Captain MacDonald, presumably sometime in the 1870s.

There is an interesting inland record of a bird on Lochs Fada and Leachan on 1.4.1968 and a further bird was present off Pabay during April 1972. It was recorded during the 1981-83 *Winter Atlas*, but no further details are available. As far as can be established, there have been no recent records, although there is a report of a 'possible' bird at Loch Cleat, Duntulm, on 19.3.2003.

SLAVONIAN GREBE   *Podiceps auritus*

Winter visitor in small numbers.   **Amber list species.**

Though Macpherson did not see the species he provides 3 records: the first was undated at Dunvegan Loch; the second was a single at Claigan on 19.12.1892;

the third was in January 1894. All were shot and mounted. Baxter & Rintoul do not add to this. Single birds were recorded off Pabay by Henson in 1956 which is probably the first indication that Skye had a small wintering population.

There were further records in the *Scottish Bird Report* in 1971 and 1972 but it was not until Ellis's winter survey of 1978/79 that the significance of these numbers was realised when birds were recorded from October to March, the best counts being 11 between Loch na Cairidh and Sligachan in December, and an exceptional 23 in the same area in Feb/March. The species was recorded from 5 squares during the 1981-83 *Winter Atlas*. During the 1984/85 winter survey of coastal birds only a single record was obtained for the Skye coast which is perhaps a reflection on observer coverage on a species which can be elusive. A report of 4 at Loch Pooltiel on 25.4.1988 is unusual.

Though small numbers continue to winter on the sheltered east coast of Skye between Portree and Kyleakin the peak numbers recorded in 1978/79 have not been surpassed. More recent maxima include 8 opposite Breakish on 1.4.1998, 8 in the greater Broadford Bay on 15.12.2001, and 10 there on 9.2.2003, 9.3.2004 and 11.2.2005, and 13 on 21.2.2007. There were 14 between Camas na Sgianadin and Loch Ainort on 26.1.2006, and in the greater Broadford Bay area on 14.1.2008. All records are from the sea lochs so a single bird on Loch Mealt on 23.9.2001 was interesting. The Pabay Sound is well favoured and smaller numbers are usually present in Loch Ainort. Birds tend to arrive in October and depart in April although WeBS counts in Broadford Bay tend to fluctuate, suggesting that the small wintering population may range over a larger area including the west coast mainland. The origins of the birds wintering on the Skye coast are not known. The species also breeds in Iceland and Thom suggested that some of the Scottish wintering population may originate in Iceland or Norway.

BLACK-NECKED GREBE   *Podiceps nigricollis*

Scarce autumn and winter visitor.   **Amber list species.**

Macpherson provides what seems an authentic account of a bird shot at Waterstein on 22.1.1895. There was apparently another bird near Dunvegan at the same time and both occurrences had followed a heavy gale.

A single on the sea at Teangue, Sleat, on 20.8.1969 is the only other record (*SBR*).

NORTHERN FULMAR   *Fulmarus glacialis*   Fulmair (eun-crom)

Breeding resident. Occurs in large numbers during passage.

Gray's suggestion that Captain Cameron of Glen Brittle 'had eggs' on Skye, where it bred on a stack off Talisker, is extremely interesting given the later information from Baxter & Rintoul, and it is perhaps significant that

Macpherson makes no reference to this record, providing only accounts of dead birds washed ashore. Specific dates of the colonisation of Skye are difficult to pin down though Sillar & Meyler appear to have gleaned information from Seton Gordon. They suggest it was seen prospecting Lord MacDonald's Table in 1933 and first bred on Skye in 1934. Seton Gordon certainly made no mention of breeding Fulmars when *In The Highlands* was published in 1931. Temperley saw birds off the cliffs at Hallaig, Raasay, in 1936, but there was no evidence of breeding. By 1946 Sillar & Meyler suggest a colony had been established at MacLeod's Maidens and along the coast nearby. It was also present on Tulm Island in 1948. Baxter & Rintoul appear to have been unaware of this data, generalising that colonisation of the Inner Hebrides was 'rather late' and that, along with other islands in the group, breeding had been proved by 1945. Writing in 1954, Murray stated that a few pairs bred and the species was increasing.

By the time of the 1968-72 *Atlas* breeding was confirmed from 17 coastal squares, predominantly in the north and west of the island and by 1988-91 this expansion had continued into a further 4 squares. During the 1981-83 *Winter Atlas* it was recorded in 8 squares, all in the north of the island. In north-west Scotland there was a population increase of 36% between 1968 and 1987. In Skye the increase was significantly greater according to Lloyd *et al.* (1991), from 1421 pairs to 6382 pairs, the majority of which are in colonies in the north and west of Skye, the largest of which are in the vicinity of Rubha Hunish. However, this figure was adjusted to 4726 following the Seabird 2000 census, suggesting a decline. Despite this, the species is currently extending its range in areas such as Strathaird and Sleat.

Burton *et al.* found significant concentrations of birds in the north of Skye and the Inner Sound during their survey in August 1986. After they fledge, young Fulmars will spend up to 4 years at sea during which time they will range extensively in the east and west Atlantic as well as the Arctic, Norwegian and Barent Seas. Though a number of adults will remain in the vicinity of their breeding colonies throughout the year, there is a marked absence of birds on Skye between November and February. A significant passage can occur offshore, e.g. 1200 were observed flying north in 2 hours at Neist Point on 30.9.1978. Also at Neist a 'Blue' was recorded travelling south on 9.10.1978.

GREAT SHEARWATER   *Puffinus gravis*

Scarce vagrant – historical record only.

Macpherson found a dead specimen among the rocks at Lowergill on 13.7.1885. Comparing this with skins of Manx and other factors, he was confident it was of this species. Apparently there had been a north-west gale a few days before which suggested it had been blown inshore. Baxter & Rintoul mention several records in the neighbourhood of Skye but do not provide details.

There appear to be no contemporary records.

SOOTY SHEARWATER   *Puffinus griseus*

Rare passage migrant.

The first record for Skye appears to be a sighting by Dr Campbell north of Rubha Hunish on 16.10.1936 (B&R).

There were a number of records from Neist Point, Uig and North Skye generally between 1976 and and 1986, all obtained between August and October, but small numbers only. A single at Braes on 27.8.1976 is more unusual. Numbers are regularly recorded from the Western Isles ferries in the Minch and in their 1986 survey, Burton *et al.* found birds concentrated in the Little Minch.

There appear to be few recent records from sea watching off the Skye coast, singles off Kilmaluag on 28.9.2001 and Neist Point on 23.8.2007 being the exception. However, birds continue to be seen from the Uig – Lochmaddy/ Tarbert ferry in late summer and also from whale watching cruises in Skye waters. It is thought the species may be regularly overlooked.

MANX SHEARWATER   *Puffinus puffinus*   Sgrail (sgrabair)

Common spring and autumn migrant. Regular offshore in summer. Amber list species.

It was abundant within the circle of the Inner Hebrides according to Gray. In *The Fauna*, Macpherson speculated that there were one or two nesting stations on the west coast of Skye: 'the evidence hereon is incomplete, but I have repeatedly observed them under suspicious circumstances'. In 1888 there was a note from Macpherson in *The Zoologist* that a friend, Mr. F.W.Johnson, had found the species nesting on the Skye coast and as proof of this he had been sent 'a fine nestling last August'. Johnson had apparently been looking for Fulmars at the time and was surprised to find that the Herring Gull nested on the same grassy ledges as the Shearwater – a fact entirely new to Macpherson. (It was also curious that Macpherson made no mention of burrows). The species was seen off Raasay by Collier. Baxter & Rintoul, however, quote Seton Gordon and R. C. Prideaux who say that it nests in the small islands off Skye but do not specify exactly where. Sillar & Meyler suggest it may nest in small numbers on stacks off Ollisdal, Talisker, and the smaller isles but provide no source for this.

During the 1968-72 *Atlas* it is recorded as possibly breeding in 2 squares in the north of Skye but further details are not available. In 1983 visits were made to all of Skye's offshore islands and although one contained c300 deserted burrows, these could have been occupied by either Puffins or Shearwaters (Roy Dennis pers. comm.).

In their August 1986 survey Burton *et al.* found a major concentration of birds in the Little Minch; and in the Seabirds at Sea survey, between August and October there were major concentrations of birds in the seas to the west of Skye. During late summer and autumn it is not unusual to find birds grounded on Skye, especially around towns and villages where birds are normally attracted by street lights during inclement weather. Many of these 'falls' involve juvenile birds, and these can normally be safely returned to sea after some 'highland hospitality'. For example in 1981 there were 40 birds at 7 different locations in Skye (A. Currie pers. comm.).

The case for breeding in Skye is in the author's view 'Not Proven' but the species does breed in huge numbers on nearby Rum where the population was estimated at c120,000 pairs in the Seabird 2000 survey. Smaller numbers breed on Canna and Eigg. Large rafts of birds occur off the west coast of Skye in July and August and many of the birds will be from these colonies. Large movements involving thousands of birds occur offshore, and can be observed from strategic headlands but the origins of these birds is more challenging. This is a truly pelagic species which ranges throughout the north and south Atlantic. It is normally present in waters off Skye from late March to October.

BALEARIC SHEARWATER   *Puffinus mauretanicus*

Scarce passage migrant.

The only record is a single off Elgol on 31.12.1994 which was originally recorded in the *HBR* as a Mediterranean Shearwater of the genus *balearicus* but is now listed as the Balearic Shearwater. This was an unusual record in itself, but given the date was even more exceptional. It was seen by a 'distinguished' group of visiting birders who I am assured are of temperate habits!

EUROPEAN STORM-PETREL   *Hydrobates pelagicus*   Luaireag (luch-fhairge)

Has bred. Rare passage migrant.   **Amber list species.**

According to an article in the *British Zoologist,* in August 1772 Pennant found them on the rocks called MacDonald's Tables off the north of Skye (Gearran Island in the Fladda-chùain group) where 'they lurked under the loose stones but betrayed themselves by their twittering noise'. In the *Old Statistical Account* for Kilmuir (1792) it was also said to be breeding on Fladda-chùain. There were numerous nesting places around the larger Islands such as Skye, according to Gray, who alluded to them breeding at Dunvegan Head which was similar to an earlier report by MacGillivray. However, Macpherson suggested it was nesting only sparingly on the Ascribs, blaming Puffins for the decline, as they were taking over Petrel burrows. Collier said it did not breed on Raasay but was common after heavy gales from the north. Baxter & Rintoul quote Seton Gordon that it nested in the small islands of Skye but not the main island. Seton Gordon writes fairly extensively about Storm

Petrels in *In The Highlands* and it is suspected that some of his observations were based on nesting birds in the Ascribs.

During the 1968-72 *Atlas*, breeding was suspected at South Ascrib Island but unfortunately by the time of the 1988-91 survey, this site was unoccupied. It was also unrecorded during the seabird surveys of 1969,1986/87 and 2000. It is notoriously difficult to census this species and its nest sites are also extremely vulnerable to rats and cats. This is a truly pelagic bird, only coming ashore under the cover of darkness to breed, but its current status as a breeding bird on Skye is uncertain.

It is regularly reported by fishermen during the summer months round the coast of Skye and frequently seen from the Uig – Tarbert/Lochmaddy ferry. Best counts include 10 in the Sound of Sleat on 5.7.1976 and 70 off Uig on 22.9.1986. In the Seabirds at Sea Survey in 1986, the waters to the north of Skye were important for the species during August and September and a late bird was seen on 5.11.1986. Recent records are increasing and include 8 at Waternish on 10.7.1999. In 2003 it was seen regularly from the Uig – Lochmaddy/ Tarbert ferry between june and October. It is also seen regularly in Skye waters from fishing and other pleasure boats, c30 east of Staffin Island on 26.8.07 being an example. During 2004 there were several reports during August and September including 10 off Neist Point and 16 off Strathaird Point. Many onshore sightings are influenced by prevailing weather conditions. There are several recent records in November.

LEACH'S STORM-PETREL   *Oceanodroma leucorhoa*

Scarce passage migrant.   **Amber list species.**

Gray reported a number of specimens obtained from Skye, chiefly found in November/December. Macpherson recorded only a single specimen, found dead at Loch Mór, Waterstein, in autumn 1891. During a huge wreck throughout Britain and Ireland in October-November 1952 a number were seen off the coast of Skye as well as several found dead (*SN* Vol.65 No.3).

Up until 2003 there were only three recent records, all of singles, at Rubha na h-Aiseig on 9.10.1978 (*SBR*), at Kylerhea on 3.9.1988, and off Ardnish, Broadford, on 30.10.2000. In 2003 the species was observed from the Uig – Lochmaddy ferry on several occasions with a peak count of 20 on 22.9. It is probably very much under-recorded. The nearest breeding colonies are North Rona and St Kilda but it should be seen in late summer and autumn especially during and after strong gales. During such a period of strong northerlies it was estimated that there were 25+ in Broadford Bay on 23.9.2004. On the following day 3 separate birds were seen in the greater Broadford Bay area and a dead bird was found in the village itself. It is suspected that a significant inshore movement had taken place precipitated by the northerly gales. It has been recorded regularly since, usually in small numbers.

NORTHERN GANNET　　　　*Morus bassanus*　　　　Sùlair (ansan)

Common offshore. Scarce in winter.　　　　**Amber list species.**

Macpherson suggested it was a summer visitor appearing in April and 'knocking about the Minch' the summer long. Collier saw it frequently off Raasay. Seton Gordon suggested in 1931 that Gannets habitually leave the north coast of Skye on 10.10, a factor not necessarily attributed to the weather or the scarcity of fish!

During the 1981-83 *Winter Atlas* it was recorded in 7 squares, mostly in the north of the island. However, it does tend to be scarce between November and February.

It is a familiar bird on the coast of Skye, often in impressive numbers, for example 1000 per hour were flying north at Neist Point on 30.9.1978. Up to 750 per hour have also been recorded heading north past Rubha Hunish. Another good count was 1000 near Waterstein on 15.9.1999. The nearest breeding colony to Skye is probably St. Kilda so birds seen early season may be either non-breeders or are returning to gannetries further north in the UK or in Iceland or Norway. Many Gannets also occur inshore around Skye from July to October taking advantage of rich fishings in the numerous sea lochs, especially the seasonal Mackerel runs. It is known that many fledged birds from Bass Rock fly north before turning south down the west coast of Scotland so the origins of the birds occurring locally is quite complex. Winter records are scarce, and 5 at Camas Mòr on 19.12.2003 was unusual.

GREAT CORMORANT　　　　*Phalacrocorax carbo*　　　　Sgarbh (ballaire)

Breeding resident.　　　　**Amber list species.**

According to Macpherson it was 'Resident, nesting sparingly on our coasts'. Though Collier had recorded it on Raasay he had no breeding record. Baxter & Rintoul had consulted Seton Gordon and R. C. Prideaux who were of the view that it no longer bred on Skye.

During the 1968-72 *Atlas* there is confirmed breeding from 7 squares. Approximately 60 pairs were counted during Operation Seafarer in 1969, the best colony being on An Dubh Camais. Over 20 pairs also nested on Longay. The accuracy of some of this reporting is questionable, a comment which is perhaps justified by the fact that it seems to have disappeared from 4 of these sites by 1988-91. However, it appears to have then bred in 4 new squares. It is probably most appropriate to refer to Lloyd *et al.* who suggest that there are 11 sites on Skye all of which are quite small. The total population during the 1985-87 seabird survey was c150 pairs and there was a slight increase during Seabird 2000. During the 1981-83 *Winter Atlas* it was recorded in most coastal squares. The earlier winter survey by Ellis had revealed relatively low wintering numbers with a max. of 50 birds.

There seems little doubt that there has been confusion in the reporting of this species for many years. It is significantly outnumbered by the European Shag. As a breeding species it is present on a number of offshore sites though it is not known whether there is any significant change in status. On the basis of Ellis's estimates, it may well have increased in numbers. Occasionally it can be seen seen feeding on inland lochs.

EUROPEAN SHAG *Phalacrocorax aristotelis* Sgarbh (Sgarbh-an-sgumain)

Common breeding resident.   **Amber list species.**

The species was first mentioned in the *Old Statistical Account* (1792) for Snizort in Skye. According to Gray it was found on Skye, and this was further supported

by Macpherson who regarded it as 'Resident', and named several nesting places. Macpherson also suggested that the Cormorants referred to by Martin Martin (1698), as nesting in a large cave on the south side of Loch Portree, were more probably of this species: 'the natives carry a bundle of straw to the door of the cave in the night time, and then setting it on fire, the fowls fly with all speed to the light, and so are caught in baskets laid for that purpose'. According to Martin, 'a Cormorant, which has any white feathers or down, makes good broth.' In Baxter & Rintoul, Seton Gordon referred to large colonies on the island of Wiay. Collier had found it plentiful and breeding on Raasay, later confirmed by Temperley who found it breeding along the north-west coast.

During the 1968-72 *Atlas*, breeding was confirmed from 22 squares, illustrating its wide distribution, and there was little change by 1988-91. A breeding population of 600 pairs was estimated in Operation Seafarer and this was later suggested by Lloyd *et al.* as being a significant underestimate. The 1985-87 seabird survey estimated 2522 pairs in Skye, against a Scotland wide population of 32,000 pairs. With 8% of the Scottish breeding population, Skye is therefore important for this species and there is some evidence that it continues to expand its range in Strathaird and Sleat. However, there was a significant reduction to 866 pairs during Seabird 2000, part of a general decline experienced throughout the country.

Widespread distribution was also recorded during the 1981-83 *Winter Atlas*, though the only specific winter counts appear to be those made by Ellis in the 1978/79 winter coastal survey. The max. count for the Skye coast was in midwinter with 1183 birds, the best areas being Lochs Slapin/Eishort. Counts include 252 in Staffin Bay and 276 on Lub Score on 13.2.1983. More recently there were 200 in Moonen Bay on 14.10.2000, 230 at Point of Sleat on 17.10.2003, and 300+ in Loch Bracadale on 18.12.2004.

GREAT BITTERN   *Botaurus stellaris*

Vagrant.

One was apparently shot at Skeabost in May 1867 (Gray), a record which was later confirmed in *The Fauna*. One was found in an emaciated condition near Uig in late December 2005. Taken into care it was released a few days later at Loch of Strathbeg (HBR).

CATTLE EGRET   *Bubulcus ibis*

Scarce passage migrant.

A single report from Broadford Bay on 18.5.1997 (*HBR*).

LITTLE EGRET   *Egretta garzetta*

Scarce passage migrant.

Only 3 known records of singles, at Kensaleyre between 2-7.7.1986 and Broadford Bay on 12.6.1996 (accepted by *SBRC*). Another single was at Drynoch for several weeks in December 2005 (HBR).

GREY HERON   *Ardea cinerea*   Corra-ghritheach (corra-ghrian)

Common breeding resident.

Gray was aware of several heronries and Macpherson confirms that the Dunvegan heronry contained 30-40 nests, and identified several others. Collier also found a small heronry in Raasay which was slowly being established following constant persecution. This persecution seems to have continued as Temperley suggested the permanent heronry in the Home Wood was destroyed some years prior to 1937 in the interests of game. The Dunvegan heronry seems to have been the longest established on Skye and supposedly contained 200 nests in 1913. However, when Baxter & Rintoul saw it in 1930 it had only 18 nests, and by 1937 the birds had moved to a new site. Baxter & Rintoul provided details of several other large heronries including one at Swordale which had 50 nests in 1922. There were other records from Sleat, Soay, Loch na Béiste and Raasay where a pair had nested on a flat rock. Writing in 1931 Seton Gordon suggested that birds from the heronry at Armadale habitually make the sea passage across the Sound of Sleat to the Scottish mainland to fish, a distance of 5 miles.

During the 1968-72 *Atlas*, breeding was confirmed from 16 squares but there may have been a slight decline in distribution by 1988-91. Though most heronries are located in trees, a number may also nest in rocks or on the ground and several pairs were found nesting in heather on Guillamon Island in the 1970s. Ellis's winter counts of 1978/79 recorded a peak of c180 birds for the Skye coast, with 28 being the largest count at any single location. During the 1981-83 *Winter Atlas* it was found in 24 squares. In the 1984/85 coastal survey of winter birds by Moser *et al.*, the sections covered in Skye and the small isles revealed 278 birds, a density of 3.24 per 10km stretch of coastline. The birds  were found mainly on sheltered shorelines, fed singly and showed a regular pattern of dispersion, suggesting territorial behaviour. The winter population of Herons on both Skye and on the western seaboard is important in a UK context according to Moser. Whilst some of these wintering birds are local in origin, ringing recoveries suggest the population is augmented by birds from Norway, obviously taking advantage of our relatively frost free winters. Severe winter weather can have a significant impact on Heron populations.

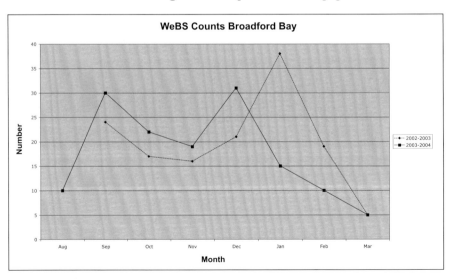

In regular WeBS counts at Broadford Bay max. counts include 23 on 8.9.2002, 38 on 11.1.2003 and 33 on 31.8.2003. Elsewhere, a count of 17 at Isle Ornsay on 28.1.2003 was interesting. These details are shown on the table on the previoous page. Both winter peaks corresponded with periods of cold weather.

WHITE STORK   *Ciconia ciconia*

Scarce passage migrant.

The only record is a single at Broadford, presumably a spring overfly, on 21.4.1977 (*SBR*).

GLOSSY IBIS   *Plegadis falcinellus*

Vagrant – historical record.

One was shot at Glen Drynoch, Skye, on 1.11.1911 (*The Scottish Naturalist*).

RED KITE   *Milvus milvus*   Clamhan gobhlach (croman)

Bred historically. Wanderers from new Scottish population occur annually. Amber list species.

Kites are included in the list for the Parish of Snizort in 1836 according to the *New Statistical Account*. Though no evidence of breeding was presented, Macpherson suggested it was resident in the south of Skye 'but nearly extirpated' and a Kite had been found nailed up by a 'keeper in 1881.

Since the reintroduction of the species in the north of Scotland there have been an increasing number of sightings of tagged birds. There was an early record at Drynoch on 2.10.1987, from Glen Brittle on 11.10.1991, and reports of birds in 1993 and several in the spring of 1995. In 1996 there were 5 separate sightings including one bird which remained in the Aird of Sleat for a fortnight. Another single was reported from the Aird of Sleat on 22.4.1997 and from Isle Ornsay on 30.4.2001. There is a report from Dunvegan on 2.8.2002, 2 records from Neist Point and Glasnakille, Strathaird, in October/ November, 2003, and a report from Ardvarsar, Sleat on 14.11.2004. The species has continued to be recorded annually.

Given that a high percentage of contemporary records are in autumn, this may suggest that some Black Isle birds disperse to the west. It is also understandable that the mixed woodland and agricultural habitats of Sleat are attractive to some of these wandering birds.

WHITE-TAILED EAGLE   *Haliaeetus albicilla*   Earn (iolair bhreac)

Bred historically. Successfully re-established as a rare breeding resident.   Red list species.

It is appropriate to quote Gray: 'The Isle of Skye may be said to be the headquarters of this conspicuous Eagle on the west of Scotland, the entire coastline of that magnificent country offering many attractions to a bird of its habits' ... 'nearly all the bold headlands of Skye are frequented by at least one pair'. However, in 9 years a single keeper on an estate shot 57 birds so it is little wonder that things deteriorated pretty rapidly afterwards and by the time Macpherson produced his manuscript for *The Fauna* there were only 'a pair or two still breeding in the south and west of Skye'. Not only were the birds being shot and poisoned but those that did manage to breed were receiving the unrelenting attention of egg collectors (see *The Fauna* for some pretty descriptive accounts). Miraculously, they managed to hang on and Baxter & Rintoul had a record of them breeding until 1916 and were told on their visit in 1930 that a pair had bred long after this, a time when they were supposedly extinct. However, no supporting evidence ever emerged after the last breeding record in Skye in 1916 and although occasional vagrant birds wandered to Scotland from Norway, to all intents and purposes the hand of man had totally eliminated the species as a breeding bird throughout Scotland.

The reintroduction project commenced in 1968 on Fair Isle but met with some initial difficulties. In 1975 the project was resumed on Rum and over a subsequent period of 20 years, 4-10 eaglets were imported annually and released. The first successful nest from the introduced stock was in 1985. This is a fascinating story which cannot be given justice in this brief summary. John Love's account, *The Return of the Sea Eagle*, published in 1983, is a wonderful read.

The first records for Skye commenced around 1978/79, most of the reports being of juvenile birds. White-tailed Eagles do not normally breed until they are 5-6 years old and the first breeding attempt in Skye was in 1986. This attempt failed and it was not until 1989 that this particular pair produced their first young. Meanwhile, another pair attempted to breed in 1987 and successfully fledged 2 young the following year. By 2007 there were 11 occupied territories on Skye. The number of breeding pairs in Scotland has slowly increased and in 2007 there were 45 territorial pairs. Young birds are fitted with colour marked wing tags and details of sightings should be passed to the RSPB.

Going back to Gray's comments in 1875, it is not surprising that White-tailed Eagles have returned to breed in Skye, although there is little evidence that they have returned to historical territories. Nonetheless it is still possible to see these majestic birds returning to the coastlands from which they were so ignominiously slaughtered. It is equally possible to see the species at virtually any viewpoint on the island, be it flying over the centre of Portree, from various roadside lay-bys, or from many of our mountain and coastal paths. The new population of birds is much less wary of man than Golden Eagles and long may their trust be rewarded. The RSPB monitor the population and have installed a video link to a nest site from which live pictures are beamed back to a viewing facility in the Aros Centre in Portree. There are also boat trips operating from Portree harbour and the local pair can regularly be seen taking fish.

EURASIAN MARSH HARRIER   *Circus aeruginosus*   Clamhan-loin

A scarce vagrant.   **Amber list species.**

The Fauna records a bird killed on Scalpay, presumably in the latter part of the 19th century and this appears to be the only historical record.

There are only three contemporary records known, with singles, at Elgol on 14.5.1994 (*HBR*) and near Glen Brittle on 23.4.2001(both K. Nellist), and a female at Ardnish, Broadford on 21.05.2008. (A & E Horner)

HEN HARRIER   *Circus cyaneus*   Brèid-air-tòin (clamhan nan cearc/luch)

Breeding resident. Passage migrant.   **Red list species.**

It was a very common species on the Inner Hebrides including Skye where it was known by its Gaelic name *Clamhan luch* (mouse hawk) according to Gray. According to *The Fauna* the species became much rarer as a result of persecution in the north-west Highlands between 1880-1900. Although described as 'Resident' on Skye it was clearly not immune from persecution and Macpherson reflected disconsolately 'presently a new generation of keepers will have sprung up who will know no more of the Hen Harrier than of the Gyr-falcon or other rare visitor.' According to Collier, prior to his time, as many as 6 pairs had nested regularly on the moors of Raasay but it had been exterminated in the interests of game and by 1899 was reduced to an occasional visitor. Baxter & Rintoul saw a bird on their visit to Skye in May 1930, but provide no further details. It may therefore still have been breeding at a time when it was long extinct elsewhere. However, Seton Gordon writing in 1931 suggested that it did not nest on Skye but that migrants from the north visited the island each autumn.

During the 1968-72 *Atlas* there were few records and it was only confirmed to breed in one square. Coverage was certainly improved by 1988-91 when it was found in 9 squares, a significant improvement, either in distribution, or in observer cover! During the 1981-83 *Winter Atlas* it was recorded in 9 squares.

A study of breeding Hen Harriers by the author commenced on Skye in 2000. The majority of nesting Harriers use forest plantations even where these are up to 25 years old. Though the study is in its infancy, wet weather early in the breeding season may considerably impact upon breeding performance. The best results were achieved in 2004 when 7 successful pairs produced 23 fledged young. Though it is difficult to assess the size of the breeding population it is likely to be in the range 15-25 pairs and therefore significant in terms of the overall Scottish population, which still faces major threats from persecution.

The size of the wintering population is equally difficult to assess and it is thought that most juveniles, as well as some adults, migrate in the autumn. Some birds seen in autumn and spring will also be migrants from populations further north. Harriers are known to roost communally outwith the breeding season and a small roost was located in north Skye in November 2004. It is used most winters and has held a maximum of 14 birds making it one of the largest roosts in Scotland.

NORTHERN GOSHAWK   *Accipiter gentilis*   Gos-sheabhag

A scarce vagrant.

According to *The Fauna* this was not a common species anywhere in the north-west Highlands, including Skye, where Macpherson regarded it as resident, but decidedly scarce.

There have only been a few recent reports, all of single birds: from Dalavil on 5.6.1988; a male recorded in north-west Skye on 23.3.1994; an adult female reported on 13.4.1995; a report from Score Horan on 11.4.1996; from Glen Brittle on 3.10.2000; from Ord on 24.3.2003 and from Camus Croise in Sleat on 17.9.2004. There is every likelihood that this species is under-recorded on the island and is now recorded annually.

EURASIAN SPARROWHAWK   *Accipiter nisus*   Speireag (speir-sheabhag)

Common breeding resident.

It was a scarce bird according to Macpherson, but bred at Dunvegan in 1885. Collier reported it as common and breeding on Raasay but there were no later records. Miss Baxter (of B&R) recorded it at Flodigarry in winter.

Confirmed breeding in only 4 squares during the 1968-72 *Atlas* and if anything the situation was even poorer by the time of the 1988-91 *Atlas* survey. Distribution during the 1981-83 *Winter Atlas* was improved with records from 14 squares.

Given the extent of recent afforestation on Skye it is not surprising that this species is well established as a breeding resident. Work carried out under the auspices of the Highland Raptor Study Group in 2002 suggests a mean brood size of 4.4 fledged chicks per nest, which compares favourably with the rest of the Highlands. It is difficult to assess the size of the breeding population but it has probably increased significantly during the last 20 years.

COMMON BUZZARD   *Buteo buteo*   Clamhan (gearr-chlamhan)

Common breeding resident.

Gray suggested it was still found in some numbers in the Inner Hebrides in the 19th century and though described in *The Fauna* as resident, it clearly had a limited distribution. Though Collier knew of only one pair on Raasay at the turn of the 19th century, Temperley reported 5 or 6 pairs breeding by 1936/37. In 1930 Baxter & Rintoul found it nested not uncommonly on Skye.

Present in every square during the 1968-72 *Atlas* and little change in 1988-91. It was also well distributed in winter with records from most squares during the 1981-83 *Winter Atlas.*

It is thought many young birds disperse in the winter months, but return to their natal areas to breed. Evidence from ringing recoveries suggests adults are largely sedentary. There is only limited knowledge of breeding success on Skye but in 1991, of 12 pairs checked, 11 were successful with a productivity of 1.5 chicks per nest (HRSG Report). This is relatively low but probably

81

reflects that the population has reached an optimum level. However, though Buzzards are well distributed on Skye, this is by no means uniform, and greatest breeding densities are probably determined by the availability of prey, especially rabbits. It is not unusual to see small groups soaring in favourable weather conditions, and a group of 9 were observed at Kilmaluag on 28.9.2001.

ROUGH-LEGGED BUZZARD   *Buteo lagopus*   Bleidir tònach

A scarce winter visitor.

According to Macpherson an example of this species was 'obtained' at Portree Lodge in October 1888.

Singles at Kensaleyre 14-18.12.1978 and Glendale on 12.4.1998 (*SBR*) appear to be the only recently accepted records. There are further reports from Skeabost on 7.10.1983, Camusunary on 16.10.1984 and Loch Eynort on 24.1.1985 but the status of these records is not known.

GOLDEN EAGLE   *Aquila chrysaetos*   Iolair dhubh (iolair bhuidhe)

Breeding resident.   **Amber list species.**

In a historical context it was probably not as common on Skye as the White-tailed Eagle, according to Gray, who was quoting Captain Cameron of Glen Brittle. In 1867 Cameron had written to say that of 65 Eagles he had killed or 'caused' to be killed, only 3 were Golden Eagles – the bird was seen as a 'pride and pest' of the parish! The account in *The Fauna* of its ongoing persecution makes for pretty depressing reading and that it survived as a breeding resident seems little short of miraculous. Collier found only immature birds on Raasay, a fair reflection that persecution was taking place. It appears that Temperley did not see the species during his stay in Raasay, implying that recent reports were probably as a result of people getting confused with Buzzards! The Raasay keepers were clearly still doing their destructive work! Perhaps for obvious reasons, Baxter & Rintoul said 'it never seems to have been an abundant bird on Skye but it had nested there regularly and it still continues to nest in small numbers'.

Golden Eagles have been studied intensively on Skye for over 25 years by K. Crane and K. Nellist. An account of this study, *Island Eagles*, was published in 1999. They estimate that there are 30-32 breeding pairs of Golden Eagles on Skye as well as a number of non-breeding, sub-adult birds. The population density is one of the highest in Scotland, which reflects the availability of food supply, and the absence of persecution. Up to 2001 an average of 18 young were fledged annually, a success rate of approximately 0.58 per territorial pair. However, breeding performance has steadily decreased since and this is a cause of concern. The number of breeding pairs has also reduced.

Year	Pairs	Nesting Attempts	Incubating	Chicks Fledged
95	31	30	23	20
96	32	29	28	19
97	32	29	28	13
98	32	27	27	24
99	31	28	27	17
00	31	28	28	17
01	31	29	26	14
02	31	28	26	17
03	31	26	26	16
04	31	27	26	17
05	31	27	23	16
06	31	27	20	11
07	29	22	20	9
08	29	25	24	17

These figures are for Skye and Raasay.
Nesting attempts = incubating or sites where birds were seen mating and nest building or where we found a prepared nest.

(Source: Crane & Nellist 2008)

Observations by Crane and Nellist suggest that adult survival rate is high, birds being known to reach 30+ years of age. An area of the Cuillin massif extending to 30,000 hectares, which supports 8 pairs of Golden Eagles, has been designated as a Special Protection Area (SPA) for the species.

The Irish Golden Eagle Reintroduction Project commenced in 2001 and a number of young birds have been removed under licence from eyries in Skye. In 2007 a young male from Skye was part of the first successful breeding of this re-introduction, a fine example of the 'celtic connection' working for conservation, and helping this magnificent species regain a foothold in territories where it was unfortunately persecuted to extinction in the early part of the 20th century.

OSPREY *Pandion haliaetus* Iolair uisge (iolair iasgaich)

**Historical breeding status unknown. Wandering birds occur annually.
Amber list species.**

A 'casual visitant' according to Macpherson, two were shot in 1878, at Loch
Bracadale and Ullinish. There is also an observation of a bird fishing Loch
Coruisk in the summer of 1883 and carrying a fish to a rock where the observer
thought it had a nest. However, there is no evidence to support this and given
that Coruisk was a popular spot even at that time, it is reasonable to assume
a nest might have been found by others, especially given the activities of
'eggers' in the late Victorian period.

Since the re-colonisation of the 1960s Osprey numbers have risen significantly
and there are currently 75 pairs breeding in the Highlands and a similar
number of pairs in other parts of Scotland. Though there has been a steady
increase in breeding numbers, the spread to the Western Highlands is fairly
slow. Whether conditions are right for colonisation of Skye is difficult to
assess given our weather conditions. The most likely factor would be the
colonisation of the nearby mainland, as breeding performance appears to be
best when breeding density is relatively high and birds can interact.

Given the size of the Scottish population it is surprising that Skye records
appear to be very limited. Probably the first record in 100 years was 2
adults recorded at Rhenetra on 14.6.1981. It was subsequently recorded
near Raasay House in May/June 1982 (per A. Currie), and north Skye on
15.7.1985. There appears to be a break in records until there were records
from Greshornish on 10.4.1998 and Idrigill on 8.6.1999. There is a report
from Kinloch, Sleat, on 5.6.2002 and birds are now recorded annually.

COMMON KESTREL *Falco tinnunculus* Deargan allt (clamhan ruadh)

Breeding resident. Passage migrant. **Amber list species.**

It was regarded as abundant on all the Inner Hebrides by Gray. Although
The Fauna stated the species was resident, there was no comment on its
abundance or distribution. Collier found it plentiful on Raasay. On the other
hand Baxter & Rintoul found it 'not uncommon' and it was also resident and
breeding on Raasay.

Well distributed in the 1968-72 *Atlas* though seemingly absent from the
Cuillin massif. Reed *et al.* described the species as especially common on
Skye. Unfortunately by the time of the 1988-91 *Breeding Atlas* there is a
marked decline, a pattern experienced in much of the north-west of Scotland,
probably related to food supply. During the 1981-83 *Winter Atlas* it had been
recorded in 19 squares, which tends to suggest that wintering birds move into
the area, albeit in small numbers.

Though no specific studies have been carried out on Kestrels, general field work on other raptors suggests that the species has a patchy distribution and it is probably more common in the north of the island. Most of the nests found have been on crags up to 1000 feet and territories appear to be large, which might reflect food shortages. Kestrels are absent from many areas under afforestation. Elsewhere in Scotland, Kestrels will use a variety of nest sites, including old crow's nests. There is certainly no shortage of crow's nests on Skye but little evidence that Kestrels have exploited this opportunity.

MERLIN   *Falco columbarius*   Mèirneal (seabhag ghorm an fhraoich)

Breeds – mainly summer visitor. Passage migrant. Amber list species.

It was commonly distributed on the west of Scotland extending to all the Hebrides, according to Gray. Similarly, Macpherson regarded it as 'Resident, generally distributed, but not very plentiful.' Collier found one or two pairs on Raasay though Temperley said later it was just a visitor. Baxter & Rintoul found them on Skye in small numbers.

It was confirmed as breeding in only one square in the 1968-72 *Atlas*, though it probably bred in 5 others. Reed *et al.* suggested that it bred on Skye only where there was open moorland. There was also an apparent decrease in records by the time of the 1988-91 *Breeding Atlas*. This species is largely migratory and it is not surprising that it was only recorded in 4 squares during the 1981-83 *Winter Atlas*. As Icelandic breeding birds are wholly migratory the origins of these wintering birds is interesting.

The Merlin is an extremely elusive species. However, in terms of nesting it shows great site fidelity. Records provided by K. Crane & K. Nellist, dating back over the last 25 years, show a wide distribution on the island with nesting taking place in deep heather banks, on crags and in old crow's nests. Other records obtained more recently support this general distribution, and in 2002 and 2003 nests were found in old crow nests in forest plantations, reflecting the species' ability to adapt to new habitats. It has also been proved to breed on Raasay. It is difficult to assess the size of the Skye breeding population as a great deal more census work requires to be done. However it is speculated that the population could number 30-40 pairs which is quite significant in terms of the overall UK population.

EURASIAN HOBBY   *Falco subbuteo*   Gormag

A scarce vagrant.

Though Macpherson quoted correspondence regarding the possible nesting of the Hobby in Skye this was rejected later by Baxter & Rintoul.

A bird was seen hunting hirundines at a site in Skye in June 2002 and another bird was seen and photographed on 21.6.2008. These are the first authenticated records for Skye. This species has now been recorded breeding in the Highlands of Scotland. Though there is a view that the habitat and weather of Skye would be unsuitable for Hobbies, the location of these sightings is being kept confidential at this time.

GYR FALCON   *Falco rusticolus*   Seabhag mhòr (seabhag ghèarr)

A scarce winter visitor.

Harvie-Brown referred to two species in *The Fauna* namely the Iceland Falcon *F.r.islandicus* and the Greenland Falcon *F.r.candicans*. This separation was largely based on plumage colour, assuming it to be predominantly white in Greenland, and darker in Iceland and Scandinavia. This separation was also continued by Baxter & Rintoul. Thom subsequnetly clarified that plumage was not a reliable indicator of origin. It has also been established that Icelandic and Scandinavian birds are largely non-migratory, suggesting that many of the early Scottish sightings may be birds from high arctic Greenland, some of which are known to reach Iceland in winter. It is therefore now appropriate to regard all historic sightings as Gyr Falcons.

It is reasonable to accept a number of records in *The Fauna* as Gyr Falcons, including a bird shot at Waternish in 1884, where another was 'obtained' in 1896. Collier saw a bird on Raasay in 1896. There was a report from Glen Drynoch in 1900, and another bird apparently overwintered in 2 successive years, 1901/02 and 1902/03, at Strathaird. Despite the explanation in the preceeding paragraph, all these sightings were correctly identified at the time as the Greenland race. The only exception was an immature Iceland shot at Waternish in March 1886 by Captain MacDonald who, unfortunately, seems to have been rather too good a shot.

The only contemporary record is of a white phase adult at Trotternish on 17.6.1984.

PEREGRINE FALCON   *Falco peregrinus*   Seabhag-ghorm (seabhag sealgair)

Breeding resident.   **Amber list species.**

The royal and noble status of the Peregrine is reflected in the 15th century charters for Dunvegan where it was known to nest. Gray regarded the species as being more plentiful on Skye than on neighbouring islands. In Macpherson's account in *The Fauna* he admits his 'notes are largely a melancholy record - in fact an obituary. I have notes on the deaths of many Peregrines.' The sad tale of persecution continues. Raasay was apparently famous for its Peregrines and Collier found a breeding pair there. Temperley thought they were still breeding on Raasay in 1936/37.

It was confirmed to breed in 6 squares during the 1968-72 *Atlas* and there seemed to be little change by 1988-91. During the 1981-83 *Winter Atlas* it was recorded in 11 squares.

This species has been subject to monitoring as part of national surveys every 10 years, following the work of Dr Derek Ratcliffe (1993). Macpherson had earlier named 15 nesting places and in 1962 Ratcliffe followed these up as well as visiting other likely cliffs, the results being only 2 nesting pairs and territories with single birds. The 1971 survey located Peregrines in 5 out of 11 territories but in 1981 there were only 6 occupations out of 14. In 1991, 23 known sites were checked (note there may be more than a single site in a territory), 3 being occupied by a single bird and 5 by a pair, 3 of which bred successfully producing 5 young (HRSG Report 1991). The occupancy of known sites in Skye was only 22%, the lowest in the Highlands. During the national  survey in 2002 only 12 territories, which had been randomly selected, were examined. Single birds were occupying 2 of these sites and another 2 were occupied by pairs which successfully fledged 4 young. Ratcliffe had expressed the view that there had been a slight and slow increase since the population crash of the 1950s but there is little evidence that this has been sustained. It remains an uncommon breeding bird on Skye and the population may never have fully recovered from earlier persecution in the Victorian era and the problems caused by the effects of agricultural pesticides between 1956-63.

The overall results of the 2002 Peregrine census show that declines in north and west Scotland, first noted in 1971, have continued. A 30% decline was noted in the Highland Region between 1991 and 2002 so the findings in Skye are consistent with this. These declines are attributed to food shortages possibly associated with changing land use. In coastal areas, marine pollution has also been suggested as a reason for declines. Fortunately, there is no longer any evidence of persecution on Skye.

WATER RAIL   *Rallus aquaticu*   Snagan allt (snagan dubh)

Rare winter visitor.   **Amber list species.**

Gray suggested that he had received 'examples' from Skye and Macpherson refers to several records, the most specific being a bird shot at Braefasach on 16.12.1890. It was rare on Raasay according to Collier, but exceptionally, 6 were shot in the winter of 1899. According to Baxter & Rintoul it was rare on Skye in winter.

There is no record during the breeding season. There were no records during the 1981-83 *Winter Atlas*. However, a bird was seen in Tokavaig, Sleat, on 12.12.1984, and another at nearby Ord on 28.2.1986.

Normally a winter visitor, a bird killed after flying into overhead wires at Isle Ornsay, Sleat, on 26.8.2002, was an interesting record. Numbers appear to vary each winter and the winter of 2002/03 seems to have been exceptional with reports from Broadford, Ose, Portree and Drynoch. There were 2 reports in early 2004 at Harrapool and from Raasay.

SPOTTED CRAKE   *Porzana porzana*   Traon bhreac

Very rare summer visitor.   **Amber list species.**

The first record appears to be a single bird calling at a location in north Skye on 30.5 and 2.6.1995. Since then birds have been reported calling in some years although as far as can be established, breeding has not been proved. The most recent report is of a bird outside Elgol on 20.6.2003 which literally ran up the car windscreen of two visiting birdwatchers (see *HBR* 2003).

CORNCRAKE   *Crex crex*   Trèan-ri-trèan (ràc an arbhair)

Summer visitor which breeds in small numbers.   **Red list species.**

Macpherson regarded it as a summer visitor and although he referred to a number of breeding records local to him, made no comment on the species' wider distribution. On Raasay Collier said it was very plentiful, 'every small field has its pair and even on the moor and foreshore there are scattered couples'. It subsequently rapidly decreased as Temperley found only a few pairs in 1936/37. Baxter & Rintoul found it on Skye in 1910 and in 1930 they found it common at Broadford and also breeding at Armadale. By the 1950s they reported that it was still breeding regularly on Skye but not in any great numbers.

During the *Atlas* years 1968-72, breeding was confirmed in 5 squares and probable breeding in 20 others, so the species was obviously still well distributed. During census work in 1978-79 there were calling birds in

31-34 territories according to Thom. In 1980 12 pairs were located by B. Philp. However, by 1988-91 there was a significant decline when it disappeared from half of its formerly occupied *Atlas* squares on Skye, a position which was also reflected throughout the rest of the UK.

Recent counts of singing males were as follows:

1988	1992	1993	1994	1995	1996	1997	1998	1999	2000	2001	2002	2003	2004	2005	2006	2007
27	15	8	9	9	2	23	12	16	23	21	23	23	32	27	16	18

According to the RSPB the population was relatively stable between 1996 and 2003 at around 21-24 pairs, which are mainly in the north of the island in the Waternish/Trotternish areas. To encourage Corncrake friendly practices, a Grassland Scheme was launched in 1996 and has involved up to 40 participating crofters covering an area of 180 hectares. More recently the numbers of participants and areas covered has decreased. Nonetheless, in 2003 12 singing males were recorded in or near sensitively managed fields participating in the scheme and the significant increase in 2004 and 2005 was extremely encouraging. However, the number of calling birds has reduced since.

COMMON MOORHEN   *Gallinula chloropus*   Cearc-uisge

Scarce breeding bird. Rare winter visitor.

This would always appear to have been a scarce species, Macpherson quoting only a handful of reports. According to the *New Statistical Account* it was reported in the Broadford area of Skye and a breeding report from Loch Cill Chriosd in 1886 confirms this. It may also have bred at Loch Eishort in 1888. *The Fauna* also refers to an attempt by Captain MacDonald at Waternish to introduce the species and a pair bred there in 1889. According to Collier, 2 pairs bred on Raasay, though they did not winter there. Temperley still found them on Rassay in the mid 1930s. Baxter & Rintoul found them breeding at Loch Cill Chriosd and near Dunvegan in 1930.

During the 1968-72 *Atlas* there were only records from 2 squares where it probably bred, but by 1988-91 it appeared to have disappeared as a Skye breeding bird. Thom stated that it bred regularly in small numbers on Skye but this may have been an overestimate. It appears to have disappeared from Lewis and Harris at much the same time, a decline attributed to mink, to which the species is extremely vulnerable.

Birds were seen at a loch in the Dunvegan area in 1993 and 1994 including a count of 6 on 17.10.1993, a probable indicator of breeding. A single bird was recorded in Raasay on 29.12.1994. A pair was back at the loch in the Dunvegan area in 2001 and a single bird was recorded on 6.10.2002. On 11.10.2003 6 birds, comprising 2 adults and 4 juveniles, were seen on the same loch. It is suspected that this had been a successful late brood.

Occurrences elsewhere appear to be in winter with 2 at Portree on 29.10.1982, a single at the River Drynoch on 28.12.2000, a single at Broadford during November 2002 and 2 there on 9.1.2003. There were singles at Waterloo, Broadford, on 26.11.2003, at Harrapool on 25.1.2004 and Loch Cill Chriosd on 16.8.2004. These observations are included to underscore the scarcity of records for the species on Skye.

COMMON COOT *Fulica atra* Lach a' bhlair (eun-snàmhach)

Bred formerly. Rare winter visitor.

According to Gray, Skye was frequented by considerable numbers but this was not confirmed by Macpherson, who provided only a handful of records, including a breeding record at Loch Waterstein (Mòr) in 1883 and Loch Cill Chriosd in 1889. Collier said it was sparingly seen on Raasay during the autumn and winter. In 1930, Baxter & Rintoul still found them breeding at Cill Chriosd.

It was not recorded during the 1968-72 or the 1988-91 *Atlas* surveys. There are records from 2 squares in the north-west of the island during the 1981-83 *Winter Atlas* and these may have been weather related movements from the population on the Uists.

It seems that there are no further records for 20 years until 1.12.2003 when a single bird was observed, remarkably enough, back on Loch Cill Chriosd where it remained for several weeks. Single birds have been recorded annually since.

COMMON CRANE *Grus grus*

Rare and accidental passage migrant. **Amber list species.**

The only accepted record is 4 at Dunvegan on 15.10.1990 (*SBR*).

EURASIAN OYSTERCATCHER *Haematopus ostralegus* Gille Brìghde (uiseag na tràighe)

Common breeding resident, passage migrant and winter visitor.
Amber list species.

According to Macpherson it was resident, nesting on low islands and less frequently on precipitous stacks. It bred commonly on Raasay according to Collier. Baxter & Rintoul saw them commonly in 1910 and 1930 and they were also said to breed plentifully on Raasay.

It was widely distributed as a common breeding bird at the time of the 1968-72 and 1988-91 *Atlas* surveys. During the 1981-83 *Winter Atlas* it was widely

distributed, but in small numbers. No estimate of either breeding or wintering numbers has been made but it is by far the commonest wader. During the winter survey of 1978/79 Ellis recorded a max. of 1100+ in the February/March count. As the species breeds extensively in Iceland and the Faeroes many of these birds are likely to occur on passage and some may winter. Reed *et al.* suggested a winter/passage min./max. for the island as 700/1260 and this probably remains accurate.

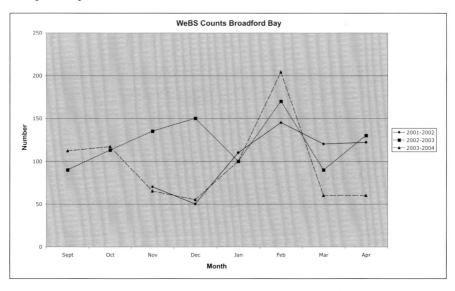

The current breeding position appears to be unchanged with breeding pairs distributed regularly along suitable areas of coast. Unlike the position on the mainland there is very little evidence that the species is breeding away from the coast. Small flocks can be found feeding on rocky shores throughout the coast both in summer and winter. However the biggest numbers favour areas with suitable inter-tidal areas of mud and sand. The best areas are Portree Loch, Loch Ainort and the greater Broadford Bay area. Peak numbers probably occur in July and August when there is a heavy passage through the area. Best counts include 300 at Broadford Bay on 11.8.2002, 500 on 5.8.2003 and 535 on 31.7.2004. In regular WeBS counts in Broadford Bay the mean count during the 2002/03 winter was 135 with numbers starting to increase in February as spring migrants return. The detail of these regular counts over recent winter periods is shown below. Whilst counts fluctuate between winters, there is a significant increase in early spring.

LITTLE RINGED PLOVER   *Charadrius dubius*

Baxter & Rintoul refer to a record of 3 on the shores of Loch Brittle on 3.6.1949 and Thom later regarded this as a somewhat strange report. The author is equally sceptical. (This species has not been included in the Skye checklist as the record cannot be validated.)

RINGED PLOVER   *Charadrius hiaticula*   Bothag (tàrmachan tuinne)

**Common breeding resident, passage migrant and winter visitor.
Amber list species.**

Macpherson regarded the species as resident and quoted several breeding records. Likewise, Collier found it breeding on Raasay, though Temperley did not find them subsequently. In 1930 Baxter & Rintoul found birds breeding in a number of places on the island.

During the 1968-72 *Atlas*, breeding was confirmed in 14 squares and it probably bred in another 7. Some decline in range was noted by the time of the 1988-91 *Atlas*. It was recorded in 13 squares during the 1981-83 *Winter Atlas*. Ringed Plover breed extensively in Iceland and Greenland and the *Migration Atlas* suggests that these populations winter in Spain and West Africa. Birds on passage may be from these populations. Reed *et al.* suggested a winter/passage min./max. for the island of 20/120 and much of this was probably based on Ellis's winter survey where the numbers found were relatively small. Given the accuracy of Ellis's counts it may be reasonable to suggest that current wintering populations are higher.

There is no apparent change in the breeding status. Peak counts occur during spring and summer migration. Spring migration occurs between March and May and counts of 33 at Claigan, Dunvegan, on 23.5.1996 and 65 at Harrapool on 30.4.2003 reflect this. Summer peaks include 60 at Ashaig on 13.8.2000, 100+ there on 25.8.2001 and 100 at Harrapool on 11.9.2004. Counts of over 50 birds have also occurred at Pool Roag and Camasunary. In regular WeBS counts in Broadford Bay counts of c50 birds have been recorded in August, September and October but normally decline to around 30 birds during the winter months. A count of 65 birds at Harrapool on 19.11.2003 and 90 on 6.1.2007 and 13.11.2007 is unusual.

EURASIAN DOTTEREL   *Charadrius morinellus*   Amadan mòintich
                                                      (gurraiceach)

Has bred. Scarce passage migrant.   **Amber list species.**

There are at least 4 records for Skye. The first was of a single on Sgurr Dearg on 7.8.1983. David Rogers had a 'trip' of 3 on the summit of Beinn na Caillich on 28.4.2000. There is also a reliable report of birds seen on Glamaig in June 2001. There is a report of 2 on The Storr on 5.5.2002. It is interesting that following what appears to be a gap of 17 years from the first report, birds are recorded in three successive years and in 2007 a nest with eggs was located. Though it is not known whether the nest was successful, it is a first breeding record for Skye.

EUROPEAN GOLDEN PLOVER *Pluvialis apricaria* Feadag (feadag bhuidhe)

Breeds. Passage migrant and winter visitor.

Gray regarded it as a resident on Skye, and Macpherson agreed, suggesting it was 'breeding numerously on our braes and broken ground'. Collier stated a few pairs bred on Raasay and he occasionally recorded flocks of 2-300 on the shore after bad weather, but presumably these birds were from elsewhere. Temperley later stated that a few pairs bred on Raasay. According to Seton Gordon in Baxter & Rintoul, it only nests sparingly on the highest hills. Writing in 1931 Seton Gordon also said that large flocks of 'northern' Golden Plover frequented north Skye in September.

Widely distributed during the 1968-72 *Atlas* with probable or confirmed breeding from 23 squares, and there was little change by 1988-91. However, this gives little indication of overall numbers although Ratcliffe (1976) had found low densities. There were a number of records during the 1981-83 *Winter Atlas*, from a total of 9 squares, all of small flocks and possibly as a result of weather movements. A count of 57 at Loch Snizort in Nov/Dec 1979 was probably exceptional as was 92 at Loch Ainort on 5.8.1987.

The Icelandic population, which numbers some 200,000+ pairs, winters in Ireland and the west of Britain and some of these birds will no doubt occur on Skye during passage.

It is difficult to assess the current breeding status of the Golden Plover on Skye. Though it is widely distributed, breeding density seems to be extremely sparse. In terms of passage flocks, the only recent counts of note was 60+ at Waternish on 13.10.2002, 60 at Camasunary on 20.10.2004, and 100 at Ramasaig on 1.11.2008. Winter counts of 36 in north Duirinish on 29.12.2002, 57 at the head of Loch Caroy on 17.1.2004 and 85 south of Uig on 20.11.2004 may reflect better observer coverage, and indicate that small flocks overwinter.

GREY PLOVER *Pluvialis squatarola* Feadag ghlas (greagag)

A regular winter visitor in small numbers. **Amber list species.**

In the winter of 1956 Henson found 2 roosting in the vegetable garden in Pabay. This appears to be the first record for Skye. A single was recorded at Portree Bay on 7.10.1973 and there was a further record of 2 at Breakish on 23.3.1979.

This is a winter visitor from Arctic Russia, which has been recorded in small numbers wintering in the Ardnish/Ashaig area of Broadford Bay during the last few years. The best count was 8 at Ardnish on 8.1.2002.

NORTHERN LAPWING *Vanellus vanellus* Adharcan luachrach (curracag)

Breeds in small numbers. Passage migrant and winter visitor.
Amber list species.

The *New Statistical Account* (1840) records them as breeding at Strath, confirmed by Macpherson who said it has long been a breeding resident on Skye, but it was local and only seemed to be recorded in relatively small numbers. Collier found it breeding on Raasay, 12-15 pairs confining themselves to a particular area when other suitable habitat was empty. It was thought unusual that the species left in autumn and there was only one November record. Writing in 1931 Seton Gordon was curious that the Lapwing was such a rare bird on Skye as there seemed to be much suitable breeding habitat. On Baxter & Rintoul's various visits they found it scarce and local as a breeding bird. According to Henson the species was extremely numerous on Pabay in summer.

Lapwings probably bred in 15 squares during the 1968-72 *Atlas* but there was some evidence of a decline by 1988-91. During the 1981-83 *Winter Atlas* it was recorded from 15 squares some of which may be interpreted as birds returning early to the breeding grounds because of favourable weather. There is little evidence of large flocks overwintering on Skye.

Best counts include 114 at Bracadale in spring 1979, and 300 at Staffin on 12.2.1980. Recent flock sizes appear to be smaller, reflecting the precarious status of the species, with 64 at Strath Suardal on 7.3.2003 and 53 at Aird Bernisdale on 30.10.2003, with similar numbers present in 2004. This latter flock may overwinter, as does a flock of 40-50 in the Harlosh area. Otherwise only small numbers are recorded during the winter months.

As far as breeding distribution is concerned this remains extremely patchy. Breeding success may be even more problematic. For example, in 2003 5 pairs bred in Strath Suardal, Broadford. All failed at their first attempt. At least 3 pairs hatched young on their second attempt and although pulli reached c2 weeks old, none fledged. Predation remains a major factor in breeding success. Apparently some 35 pairs used to breed in this area (A. Currie pers. comm.).

RED KNOT   *Calidris canutus*   Luatharan gainmhich

Regular passage migrant in late summer/autumn. Amber list species.

The earliest record is by Macpherson who saw a small group of Knot at Dunvegan in early January, 1886. Collier found it sparingly on Raasay, a single being shot for identification purposes in January 1899. Henson recorded singles on Pabay in February, 1956, and it was recorded by Ellis in the autumn of 1978.

These birds are likely to be from the population which breeds on the Canadian Arctic islands and north Greenland which winter in western Europe. Many undertake long, non-stop flights to their wintering areas, and stopovers on Skye will be brief and probably influenced by weather patterns.

It is suspected that this species may have been overlooked in the past because it is a regular passage migrant which is recorded frequently in the greater Broadford Bay area. It has also been recorded at Pool Roag, Neist Point, Strathaird Point and several other locations. Best counts in the Broadford area include 60 on 12.8.2005 and 28 on 5.08.07. Winter records are scarcer and involve small numbers.

SANDERLING   *Calidris alba*   Luatharan glas (trilleachan glas)

Regular passage migrant in late summer/autumn.

This is another long distant migrant from the high Arctic tundra. It was not recorded by Ellis during his comprehensive survey of 1978/79. Neither was it referred to by Lees *et al.* in *The Birds of the Inner Hebrides* (1983), though birds had been recorded earlier by T. Dix at Loch Ainort. K. Nellist observed 2 at Camastianavaig on 6.4.1988.

The majority of the recent records are from Ardnish and Harrapool near Broadford. There has only been a single spring record at Harrapool on 21.5.2002. Otherwise records are in August and September, with the best counts being 13 at Broadford on 18.8.2002, 17 on 11.8.2004, 14 on 3.8.07, and an exceptional 29 on 31.7.2008.

LITTLE STINT   *Calidris minuta*   Luatharan beag

Very scarce passage migrant.

Only a handful of records can be traced including 2 at Portree Bay on 7.10.1973, 2 at Loch Harport on 9.9.1979, an unusual count of 20 at Portree Bay on 23.7.1980 and 1 there on 24.5.1986. There is also a record from Glen Brittle on 19.9.1989. There was a single at Harrapool on 1.8.2006.

PECTORAL SANDPIPER   *Calidris melanotos*

Scarce North American vagrant.

The only record was a single at Ardmore, Waternish, on 31.8.1977.

CURLEW SANDPIPER   *Calidris ferruginea*

Very rare passage migrant.

The only known record was a single at Camas Mòr, Kilmuir, on 19.9.1993, until up to two were found at Harrapool in late May, 2007, (M. Benson).

PURPLE SANDPIPER   *Calidris maritima*   Cam-glas

Regular winter visitor in small numbers.   **Amber list species.**

According to Gray, a Dr Dewar had observed several flocks on the Ascribs on 6.5.1870. It is of interest that Macpherson also regarded the Ascribs as a favourite haunt in May. He also had several winter records from the north-west corner of Skye. Collier found it common on Raasay in winter and spring, his best count being 50 on 24.1.1899. Seton Gordon enjoyed an early morning bathe in the sea, even in winter, and writing in 1938 he recalled an incident near Duntulm where he swam towards a Purple Sandpiper on a rock, almost touching it. He suspected the bird thought he was a seal! The species was recorded on Pabay by Henson in February, 1956, with a max. count of 5.

The largest count recorded by Ellis during his winter survey was 15 at Breakish in February/March 1979 and there were also reports of flocks up to 20 being recorded at Neist Point. During the 1981-83 *Winter Atlas* the species was recorded from 4 squares, including 2 flocks of 11 or more, unusual in current experience.

Although Purple Sandpipers have been seen occasionally during the last few years, numbers appear to be small, though the species can be found at a number of scattered locations. Groups are not seen with any regularity so it is difficult to make any estimates of wintering numbers. The biggest counts have been in the Broadford Bay area where up to 25 have been seen, and a kayak trip round Pabay on 24.12.2006 found 52 birds.

DUNLIN   *Calidris alpina*   Pollaran (grailleag)

Breeds. Common passage migrant. Winters in small numbers.
Amber list species.

Though Macpherson regarded it as a casual visitor he also recorded 2 likely breeding records in 1890. Collier said it bred on Raasay. Baxter & Rintoul found several pairs breeding near Sconser in 1930.

There was no confirmed breeding during the 1968-72 *Atlas*, though it possibly bred in 2 squares. Though there were no further confirmed breeding records by 1988-91, it was recorded in 8 further squares so may well have been previously overlooked. According to T. Gerrard it bred on Pabay between 1971-81. It was recorded in only 4 squares during the 1981-83 *Winter Atlas*. Reed *et al.* suggested a max. passage/winter count of 50 but did acknowledge that flocks of up to 200 occurred.

According to the *Migration Atlas* the majority of Dunlin which breed in Britain winter further south in western Europe and west Africa. Birds occurring on passage and in winter are likely to be from the Icelandic and Greenland populations.

Little is known about the current breeding status and though numbers are thought to be sparse, there is certainly evidence that as well as breeding in upland habitats, it may also breed near the coast. Passage flocks of Dunlin are liable to be recorded anywhere along the Skye coast. The most significant numbers are recorded in the Broadford Bay area in late summer and include 200+ on 26.8.2001 and 21.8.2003, with 380 on 5.8.2006 being the best count. Best counts in spring include 55 at Loch Slapin on 2.5.2001 and 100+ at Ardnish on 16.5.2002. These later birds are liable to be high Arctic breeders and in 2003 there were 90 at Pool Roag on 6.5 and 220 at Broadford Bay on 9.5, with 250 on 24.5.2007.

Small numbers overwinter in the Broadford Bay area where the maxima rarely exceed 70 during WeBS counts.

| **RUFF** | *Philomachus pugnax* | Gibeagan |

Rare passage migrant.

It is suspected that this species may be overlooked as, surprisingly, the only records which can be traced are singles in Broadford Bay on 17.7.1986 and 8.9.2005.

| **JACK SNIPE** | *Lymnocryptes minimus* | Gobhrag bheag |

A regular passage migrant and winter visitor.

Gray stated 'it was found in small groups in the marshes'. According to Macpherson it was a winter 'visitant' and one was shot in Glendale in August, 1884. Collier found it in winter on Raasay, commenting that it managed to keep in good condition in even the hardest winter. Collier also recorded a bird on the late date of 3rd June. Seton Gordon also found the Jack Snipe in north Skye in September. Baxter & Rintoul agreed it was a winter visitor.

Ellis recorded a single at Broadford in January/February 1979. There was only a single record during the 1981-83 *Winter Atlas*. There was a record from Elgol on 31.12.1994. Between 2000-03 singles were recorded each November at Elgol, Torrin, and Broadford. In 2004 singles were recorded at Ardnish on 22.2, at Torrin on 29.2, with 3 at Isle Ornsay on 5.3 and a single there on 6.3. This flush of records may have been associated with a spell of hard weather. Birds continue to be recorded annually in winter.

This winter visitor from Siberia is probably overlooked on Skye because it sits very tight and almost needs to be stood on before it will flush. Some birds may occur on passage to Ireland where it winters in significant numbers but others may overwinter, dependent on weather conditions.

COMMON SNIPE　　　*Gallinago gallinago*　　　Gobhar/meannan adhair
　　　　　　　　　　　　　　　　　　　　　　　(naosg, budagoc, eunghobhrag)

**A common breeding resident, passage migrant and winter visitor.
Amber list species.**

In the *Old Statistical Account* (1795), it is mentioned on the Portree list,
and also for Strath in the *New Statistical Account* (1840). It was a resident,
nesting in a number of locations according to Macpherson. Collier said it bred
commonly on Raasay although Temperley later found none. Baxter & Rintoul
quote Seton Gordon that it breeds and is fairly numerous near Portree.

During the 1968-72 *Atlas* confirmed breeding was obtained in 13 squares
and an even more widespread distribution was established in 1988-91. Also
widely distributed in winter, it was recorded in 16 squares during the 1981-83
Winter Atlas. The origins of these wintering birds is interesting and birds of
Icelandic origin may be involved (Thom 1986). Lees *et al.* suggested a winter/
passage max. of only 20, which is a significant underestimate.

The Snipe breeds widely on Skye. The population which occurs on passage
and which overwinters is probably quite large as it is a species which can
be found almost anywhere where damp conditions prevail – and there is no
shortage of such conditions on Skye! Consequently, it is rarely found in large
numbers and 11 at Ashaig at a fresh spring, during frost, on 30.12.2000 is
unusual as was 20 at Struan on 20.12.2003. A group of 9 at Ardnish on
24.8.2003 was also unusual and may indicate early passage.

EURASIAN WOODCOCK　　　*Scolopax rusticola*　　　Coileach-coille
　　　　　　　　　　　　　　　　　　　　　　　(crom nan duilleag)

**Breeds. Common passage migrant and winter visitor.
Amber list species.**

Though Macpherson regarded it as a 'winter visitant' it was also noted to
breed in the Broadford area, at Armadale and on Raasay. Collier found a
significant immigration of Woodcock to Raasay in the autumn, and in the
winter of 1894/95 nearly 900 were shot, whilst the 1901/02 winter produced
a total of 496. As a keen sportsman, this led Collier to suggest that Raasay 'is
one of the most favoured spots for Woodcock, if not the most favoured of all,
in Great Britain and Ireland'. Though not on the same scale as Raasay, it was
obviously shot extensively in winter in the area, and on the Strathaird Estate
up to 50 'couples' were shot in a season in the 1920s. Writing in 1931 Seton
Gordon suggested that 'regularly about October 24 the first Woodcock reach
Skye from their Scandinavian haunts'.

The earliest estimates of the Skye breeding population were from Alexander
(1945-47) who suggested there were 115 pairs on the island. There was
either confirmed or probable breeding from 9 *Atlas* squares in 1968-72, but a

possible decline in 1988-91. During the 1981-83 *Winter Atlas* it was recorded from 13 squares. Given the comments about Raasay above, it is particularly surprising that there was no record from Raasay at this time. This may simply reflect poor observer coverage. Lees's paper probably underestimates the numbers of birds occurring on passage or wintering. For example in late February 2004 after a severe snow fall birds were recorded widely at roadsides and in gardens. The origin of many of the birds which occur on Skye is probably Scandinavia.

In conjunction with the Game Conservancy, Eilean Iarmain Estate in Sleat has been improving habitat for Woodcock both for breeding purposes, as well as for winter cover. Though Woodcock have been shot on the estate for 25 years, numbers are restricted, and on average 200 birds are shot each season between November and January. Wintering birds tend to arrive in October. Sightings of Woodcock over the past 5 seasons, out with the same team of observers on 5 comparable days, were as follows:

1999	2000	2001	2002	2003
61	43	99	111	98

The above figures are seen as reflecting good conservation and habitat improvement policies (M. Mackenzie pers. comm. and *Shooting Times & Country* magazine 14.8.2003).

BLACK-TAILED GODWIT   *Limosa limosa*   Cèarra-ghob

A regular passage migrant, usually in late summer.   Red list species.

There is no historical record which is surprising. The first record appears to be a single at Broadford on 28.8.1948. Seton Gordon reported a single at Portree in December, 1949 (*SN*). During his stay on Pabay, Henson recorded a single bird on regular dates in February and March, 1956.

During the 1980s there were only 2 reports, both from Loch Portree, 2 on 8.11.1982 and a single on 26.8.1988.

This is a species which has been regularly overlooked. There is a significant breeding population in Iceland and experience in recent years suggests that it occurs regularly on passage, especially in late summer. It has been recorded at Pool Roag, Portree Loch, Loch Ainort and especially Broadford Bay. Counts include 8 at Ashaig on 25.8.2001 and 11 at Pool Roag on 26.7.2002. 2003 was an exceptional year with birds recorded in the Broadford area from August to October with peak counts of 44 on 4.8 and 32 on 21.8. Unusually, a single bird was present at Harrapool with Bar-Tailed Godwits until the end of 2003. In 2004 there were 29 at Lower Breakish on 18.7 and 26 at Harrapool on 14.8, and similar numbers appear annually. Spring passage birds are more unusual and in 2007 there were 25 at the River Snizort on 21.4 and 21 at Waterloo on 23.4.

100

BAR-TAILED GODWIT   *Limosa lapponica*   Roid-ghuilbneach

A regular passage migrant and winter visitor.   Amber list species.

The first records for Skye were from Macpherson, in 1892 at Ullinish and on the Skinidin shore on 11.1.1889. Baxter & Rintoul simply say there are few records for Skye. Henson was the first to record any numbers, his count of roosting birds in winter 1956 peaking at 22 on Pabay.

During the 1981-83 *Winter Atlas* there were records from 3 squares, the only significant flock being at Broadford Bay.

This species is an annual winter visitor to Skye, albeit in small numbers, the limiting factor being available feeding, particularly in the greater Broadford Bay area, which it favours. It is a species which breeds on the arctic tundra. Small numbers also overwinter at Loch Portree, with a max. of 12 there on 19.11.2007. Numbers at Broadford have peaked at 25 on 10.3.2001 and 21 on 10.2.2002, remarkably similar to the numbers recorded by Henson 50 years ago.

WHIMBREL   *Numenius phaeopus*   Eun Bealltainn (guilbneich bheag)

A common passage migrant, particularly in late spring. Amber list species.

Macpherson described it as a periodical visitant, numerous on sea lochs in May, on its way to breeding grounds further north, thus living up to its name of the 'May-fowl'. Collier also found it on Raasay in May. The species is not mentioned by Baxter & Rintoul in regards to Skye.

Between 1973 and 1981 B. Philp recorded the species on a number of occasions mainly on late summer passage, the best count being 5 at Braes on 29.7.1978. It was recorded from 5 squares during the 1988-91 *Breeding Atlas* but these were probably birds passing through. Though birds breed in the north of Scotland they have never been known to breed on Skye. Lees *et al.* were unable to quantify the numbers of birds occurring on passage from the absence of data available.

There is a conspicuous passage of birds northwards in April and May through Skye. Although the return passage in late summer/autumn is less apparent, there has been an increasing number of records recently. More than 100,000 birds breed on Iceland so this population may be involved on passage to and from their wintering grounds in West Africa. During northwards passage birds can be seen almost anywhere on the coast of Skye, stopping off to re-fuel. Many birds appear to follow the coastline northwards, often singly or in small groups. The main passage commences in mid April and peaks in May. Counts include 8 at the Point of Sleat on 28.4.1996, 20 off Strathaird Point on 9.5.2003 and 45 at Harrapool on 16.5.2002. The main passage southwards commences in July and ends in September, peaking in August. Recent counts in the Broadford area include 20 on 15.8.2002, 14 on 2.8.2003 and 17 on 19.8.2003. Two of these flocks were heading south-west in the direction of Loch Slapin.

In 2003 a suspected 'late' bird was recorded on the shores of Loch Scavaig at Glen Scaladal on 9.11. What is thought to be the same bird was present at Camasunary on 6.12.2003 and on 12.2.2004. During the last two dates it was accompanied by a Curlew. Camasunary is an extremely remote location exposed to the full forces of the prevailing winter south-westerlies. That this bird was able to successfully overwinter may be further evidence of possible climate change. It appears to be one of the first occasions a Whimbrel has been proved to overwinter in Scotland. There were several November records in 2007 suggesting more birds may be wintering.

EURASIAN CURLEW   *Numenius arquata*   Guilbneach (crotach mara)

Breeds locally. A common passage migrant and winter visitor.
Amber list species.

It is mentioned for Skye in the *Old Statistical Account* (1795). Although regarded by Macpherson as a 'numerous resident', he did not find birds nesting in large numbers. Collier had found the Curlew breeding on Raasay. Baxter & Rintoul found it in 1930, but in 1946 Seton Gordon suggested that other than at Armadale, it was almost unknown as a breeding bird.

It was confirmed as breeding from 10 *Atlas* squares during 1968-72 and there was little apparent change by 1988-91. It breeds quite sparsely on Skye as in the rest of the Western Highlands. Well distributed in winter however, and in the winter survey of 1978/79 by Ellis, monthly counts on the Skye coast regularly exceeded 450. During the 1981-83 *Winter Atlas* it was found in virtually every square, though in small numbers. There is some evidence from the *Migration Atlas* that birds from both the north of Scotland and further afield in Norway, may occur in winter.

There is no recent evidence regarding breeding status. The species is well distributed throughout the coast during passage and in winter frequenting inter-tidal zones both on rocky and sandy shores, moving on to fields and open moorland to feed at high tide. Most sea lochs contain small flocks, the Snizort valley, Loch Bracadale, Loch Harport, Loch Portree, and the Broadford Bay complex being favourites. Recent counts include 130 at Portree Bay on 27.8.2001, 72 in Broadford Bay on 13.01.02 and 90 there on 14.10.2003.

SPOTTED REDSHANK   *Tringa erythropus*

Scarce passage migrant.   **Amber list species.**

The only records are of single birds at Lower Breakish on 17.2.1996 (*HBR*) and at Waterloo from 10-14.10.2008. (M.Benson).

COMMON REDSHANK *Tringa totanus*   Righ-ghuileanach (maor-chladaich)

A rare breeding resident. Common passage migrant and winter visitor. Amber list species.

Historically, this species seems to have been scarce and mainly a winter visitor, though it had been thought to breed near Broadford by Macpherson. Although Collier found it common on the coast he only knew of a single pair breeding on Raasay. Baxter & Rintoul could add little to this.

During the 1968-72 *Atlas*, breeding was only confirmed in 3 squares and this was increased slightly in 1988-91. It bred on Pabay between 1971-81. During Ellis's 1978/79 winter survey the max. monthly count for Skye was only 90. In the 1981-83 *Winter Atlas* of it was recorded in 13 squares.

It is certainly much more common as a bird of passage and in winter than it is a breeding bird. Peak passage however is likely to be in late summer and a count of 60+ in the Broadford area on 20.8.2003, 70 at Harrapool on 12.8.2004, with an exceptional 150 at Ardnish on 15.7.2008, reflect this. Elsewhere there were 50 at Pool Roag on 12.8.2004. However, overall numbers are surprisingly low, and although small flocks occur in a number of locations, wintering Redshank tend to be scattered sparsely along our coastline. It is suspected that many of these passage and wintering birds are Icelandic in origin.

COMMON GREENSHANK   *Tringa nebularia*   Deoch-bhuigh

Breeding resident, passage migrant and winter visitor.

Gray spoke of a breeding station near Sligachan frequented by 2-3 pairs. Macpherson stated 'on the whole it was a rare bird on Skye and I hope ornithologists will not come to Skye in search of it'. (He should have said egg and specimen collectors!) Macpherson did find a single bird on Pabay on 20.11.1899. Harvie-Brown goes on to say 'as an indication of the scarcity of the Greenshank in parts of Skye, I may mention that only one has been seen or shot at Strathaird during the last six years'. It was rare on Raasay being occasionally seen in autumn. Baxter & Rintoul were unable to elaborate further saying there was practically no information about its migrations on the island. Perry, however, recorded 'northing' Greenshanks near Kyleakin and also said there was a pair near the mouth of the Lorgill River in the 1940s.

Breeding was either confirmed or probable in 6 squares during the 1968-72 *Atlas* and had slightly increased in 1988-91. Reed *et al.* suggested 10-15 pairs bred on Skye. This was similar to what had earlier been suggested by Nethersole-Thompson in 1979. Data collected by the John Muir Trust between 1997 and 2002 suggested that up to 8 pairs may breed annually on the Sconser and Torrin estates alone (K. Miller pers. comm.). Several pairs have recently been located in forested areas in the north of the island, suggesting afforestation took place around what were traditional sites. What is evident from this and other recent data is that the species is much more widespread than was previously considered. It is suggested that 40+ pairs may breed in Skye and that the species may be extending its range.

It was recorded in 4 squares during the 1981-83 *Winter Atlas*, though only in small numbers, a position already established in the winter coastal survey of 1978/79 when the max. monthly count was 11. In records going back over 20 years it is evident that Greenshank have wintered on Skye in reasonable numbers and with the tendency towards milder winters it will be interesting to establish whether this is an increasing trend. The origin of these wintering birds is not known but given the size of the local population, it is evident that a significant part of this migrates south for the winter. Reed *et al.* also suggested that the max. winter/passage count was 10 which is certainly an underestimate on the basis of existing numbers. During winter, single birds tend to be scattered at a number of sites including Loch Slapin, Loch Eishort, Loch na Dal, Portree Loch and Loch Ainort. Monthly WeBS counts in the Broadford Bay complex range from 5-10 birds, and it is estimated that up to 20 birds may winter on the Skye coast.

According to Thom, movements back towards the coast start in late June, and some of these birds are females which leave the males to look after the broods. Counts in Broadford Bay of 15 on 15.6.2003, and 12 on 18.7.2004 may have comprised females or failed/non breeders. The table below reflects this and also shows the 3 year mean numbers recorded in regular monthly WeBS counts.

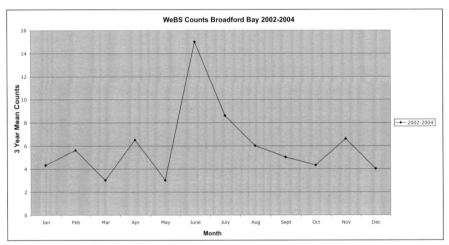

GREATER YELLOWLEGS   *Tringa melanoleuca*

Accidental North American visitor.

The only record is a single at Loch Sligachan on 19.5.1985 (*SBR*).

White-tailed Eagle chasing Great Black-backed Gull © www.skye-birds.com

Razorbills © www.skye-birds.com

Grey Phalarope © www.skye-birds.com

Redshank © www.skye-birds.com

Manx Shearwater © www.skye-birds.com

Greenshank © www.skye-birds.com

Snow Bunting © www.skye-birds.com

Dunlin © www.skye-birds.com

male Hen Harrier © www.skye-birds.com

Spotted Redshank © Martin Benson

Curlew Sandpiper © Martin Benson

Whimbrel © www.skye-birds.com

Turnstone male in summer plumage
© www.skye-birds.com

Black Guillemot © www.skye-birds.com

Brent Geese © Martin Benson

White-tailed Eagle © www.skye-birds.com

male Wheatear © www.skye-birds.com

male Lesser Redpoll in summer plumage
© www.skye-birds.com

Redwing © www.skye-birds.com

Common Buzzard © www.skye-birds.com

Ringtail Hen Harrier © www.skye-birds.com

Sedge Warbler © Martin Benson

GREEN SANDPIPER   *Tringa ochropus*

Scarce passage migrant.

The only record traced for Skye is a single at Loch Harport on 22.7.1987 (*HBR*).

WOOD SANDPIPER   *Tringa glareola*   Luatharan coille

Very rare passage migrant.   **Amber list species.**

According to Thom the species was recorded on Skye in the late 1950s but no further details were provided. There was a further record at Sron ard a'mhullaich, Loch Ainort, in 1984 (T. Dix). A bird was seen at a possible breeding site on 28.4.2007 (R McMillan).

COMMON SANDPIPER   *Actitis hypoleucus*   Luatharan (eàrr-ghainmhich)

Very common summer visitor.

It was a summer visitant, according to Macpherson, a few pairs nesting on all the lochs and burn sides. Collier found it extremely abundant on Raasay. It was later found to be very common on Skye and Raasay by Baxter & Rintoul, and also by Temperley.

The species was widely distributed as a breeding bird during the 1968-72 *Atlas*, breeding in every square. There was no apparent change by 1988-91.

In the absence of other data it is difficult to make an assessment of the current status of the Common Sandpiper. The population still appears to be strong. Birds tend to arrive in late April and most adults and their young have left by the end of July. There are no counts of any significance and 8 at Loch Slapin on 5.5.2003 followed a spell of westerlies, and may have involved migrants. There was a very late bird at Broadford Bay on 14.11.2007.

SPOTTED SANDPIPER   *Actitis macularius*

A scarce North American vagrant. Has bred.

Remarkably, a pair attempted to breed in Skye in 1975. The birds were present at least from 15.6-3.7 and laid a clutch of 4 eggs. These failed to hatch although 2 of the eggs were later found to be fertile. This was the first known breeding attempt by this North American species not just in Scotland, but in Europe and the Palearctic region.

RUDDY TURNSTONE *Arenaria interpres* Trilleachan beag (drilleachan beag)

Common winter visitor and passage migrant.   **Amber list species.**

Though not seen by Macpherson personally, others had noted it, particularly on 'vernal migration' on the Ascribs and elsewhere where a pair had been seen in full breeding plumage on 20.6.1882. The bird's actions however, suggested little other than late passage. Henson found small numbers wintering on Pabay in 1956.

There was a surprisingly limited distribution during the 1981-83 *Winter Atlas*, with records from only 4 squares. In the earlier winter survey by Ellis in 1978/79 a total of only 63 were recorded. However, this is a species which is easily overlooked and it is suggested that its winter distribution on Skye and its offshore islands is much more widespread, though flocks tend to be on the small side. It also occurs on passage. These birds are thought to originate in north Greenland and Canada.

Birds have been recorded in every month and passage birds can occur anytime between April and the end of October. The small winter flocks tend to be relatively stable. Most rocky shore sea lochs will have small groups and favoured areas include Loch Brittle, Loch Slapin, Loch Ainort, Loch Bracadale, Loch Scavaig and the Broadford Bay area. Birds will also frequent offshore islands such as Pabay. Most flocks are less than 50 and counts of 60 at Ardnish on 9.12.2006 and 52 at Loch Brittle on 31.12.2005 are exceptional.

RED-NECKED PHALAROPE *Phalaropus lobatus* Deargan allt (isean dearg)

Scarce passage migrant – historical record only.   **Red list species.**

According to Gray he obtained 'a specimen in breeding dress' from Skye. Captain Cameron had obviously told Macpherson that he had obtained a specimen in winter (which seems most improbable). Baxter & Rintoul say there is a record for Skye but do not provide details.

Although there have been a number of reports in the contemporary period, none of these were ever submitted to the Highland Recorder and therefore their status cannot be verified.

GREY PHALAROPE   *Phalaropus fulicarius*

Very rare passage migrant.

During the Seabirds at Sea survey a bird was recorded off the north-west coast of Skye on 10.10.1986 and this would appear to be the first record for Skye. Another single was seen from the ferry off Uig on 2.11.2000. There was a further record from the Point of Sleat on 17.10.2003. Though this is a scarce species, it is probably under-recorded off Skye. In October 2008 there was an exceptional influx at Camas a' Mhòr-bheòil, Gedintailor Braes. Probably weather related numbers peaked at 197 and birds remained in the area for two weeks (see HBR 2008 for summary).

POMARINE SKUA   *Stercorarius pomarinus*   Fàsgadair donn

Rare passage migrant.

Three Skye specimens of this species are in the British Museum and Harvie-Brown suggests they were probably obtained in October, 1884, near Broadford. Macpherson also records a bird from Loch Bracadale in July, 1889.

There are no further records until 1978 when P. Ellis had singles at Rubha na h-Aiseig on 9.10 and Broadford on 10.11. Bruce Philp recorded 4 from the Mallaig-Armadale ferry on 5.5.1979 and a single at Rubha Hunish on 2.5.1980. In 1983 Roy Dennis recorded 12 flying north on spring passage at Kylerhea.

There was a report of a single at Vaternish Point on 19.9.1993 (*HBR*) and a record of 5 off Soay on 17.5.2000. Singles were reported from Ashaig on 27.10.2001, Staffin Slipway on 1.10.2003 and Ardnish on 16.10.2004. There were 2 off Strathaird Point on 17.10.2004.

Following westerly gales there was an unprecedented passage of birds recorded off the west of Scotland in May 2003. Part of this spilled into Skye with a total of 33 birds recorded in Loch Slapin on 8.5. The birds were in 3 separate groups of 8, 4 (dark phase) and a large party of 21 – all in stunning breeding plumage. Smaller numbers were recorded in spring 2004. Given the earlier records by Bruce Philp and Roy Dennis, in favourable weather conditions, this species may occur on spring passage with some regularity. Small numbers occur in late Autumn and there were possibly 20 birds in Broadford Bay following northerlies on 8.11.2007.

ARCTIC SKUA   *Stercorarius parisiticus*   Fàsgadair

An occasional passage migrant from spring, more frequent late summer.

This species was also known as Richardson's Skua which was regarded by Macpherson as an 'irregular autumnal visitor' and he only mentions a few sightings. Collier said it was often seen off Raasay in the autumn.

Pete Ellis recorded singles on 4 occasions in north-west Skye in 1978. Roy Dennis recorded 4 flying north through Kylerhea on 20.5.1983.

Though there is a paucity of records from Skye, during the last 20 years it is suspected this reflects lack of coverage, as it is regularly offshore during summer and autumn. Any concentrations of Gulls and Auks which gather to feed are likely to have Skuas in attendance. During the last few years birds have been recorded regularly at Camas Mór, Point of Sleat, Strathaird Point, Neist Point, Loch Dunvegan and Broadford, mainly in singles and small groups with no significant counts of note.

LONG-TAILED SKUA   *Stercorarius longicaudus*   Fàsgadair stiùireach

A scarce passage migrant.

A specimen, referred to as a Buffons Skua, was shot in Skye in autumn 1855 (Gray) and exhibited at a meeting of the Royal Physical Society of Edinburgh. Macpherson also refers to a report of a bird frequenting Loch Sligachan in December 1890 – this is extraordinarily late and seems highly unlikely!

There have only been a handful of recent records. A single was seen flying north through Kylerhea on 20.5.1983. A single on the Uig-Tarbert Ferry crossing on 8.6.1993 is a Skye record (*HBR*). On 8.5.2003 a group of 3 were recorded in Loch Slapin along with Pomarine Skuas. In 2004 a single was recorded off Strathaird Point on 18.5 and there was a report of 2 near Kyleakin on 22.5. Birds have been recorded in most years though in small numbers.

Spring passage migrants are liable to occur with greater regularity than the record suggests.

GREAT SKUA   *Stercorarius skua*   Fàsgadair mòr (tuilleag)

Breeds. Regular passage migrant.   **Amber list species.**

Although there was obviously some difficulty differentiating species of Skua in the late 20th century, it is nonetheless surprising that the Great Skua is absent from the historical Skye record. In fact its first mention is in Baxter & Rintoul, that of a young bird ringed in south-east Iceland in August 1942 and found dead at Talisker, Skye, the following January.

This is a species which is under-recorded and is common offshore in summer and autumn – most of these birds are probably from the breeding grounds in the Northern Isles. However, it is a species which is expanding its range and has probably now bred at several locations including Fladday and Staffin Island. During the last few years non breeding birds are present widely throuhout the summer months.

Although spring records are scarce, there were 6 at Neist Point on 26.4.2000. It is regularly offshore in summer and autumn and best counts include 31 following a fishing boat off Kilt Rock on 1.9.2007. There was a late bird at Loch Slapin on 30.12.2006.

LITTLE GULL   *Larus minutus*   Faoileag bheag (crann-fhaoileag)

A rare passage migrant.

There are only 4 records. A specimen was killed by Captain Cameron of Glen Brittle in 1865 which remained the only record for the island until 2 adults were observed at Moonen Bay, Neist, on 16.5.1987. An immature was recorded at Kylerhea on 2.9.1992. A first winter bird was recorded from the ferry off Uig on 2.11.2000. There was an adult in Broadford Bay on 18.7.2007.

SABINE'S GULL   *Larus sabini*

Scarce passage migrant.

There are several records for Skye including an adult at Loch Snizort on 19.8.1979, a single off the Ascribs on 5.9.1988 and a juvenile at Staffin 20.10.1989 (all *SBR*). More recently an adult was under observation for 6 hours between Staffin Island and Flodday on 30.8.2003 (*HBR*) and there was a juvenile seen from the Uig-Tarbert Ferry on 12.9.2007. A dead adult was found at Camas Malag, Strathaird on 25.11.2008.

BLACK-HEADED GULL   *Larus ridibundus*   Ceann-dubhan (faoileag à
                                                      chinn dhuibh)

Rare breeding species. Regular on passage in small numbers.
Amber list species.

Obviously a scarce species in Macpherson's time, he had only recorded it on three occasions. Collier found it on Raasay in early summer but it did not breed. Baxter & Rintoul only state there is no breeding record for the island.

During the 1968-72 *Atlas* it was confirmed to breed in 1 square and probably bred in 3 others. Possibly the significance of these records was lost on the observers and no further details were provided. During the 1988-91 *Atlas* it was confirmed in 2 squares. Distribution was more widespread during the 1981-93 *Winter Atlas* with records from 9 squares.

Most of the records for Skye are of small numbers, 11 at Loch Portree on 2.4.1976 being above average at that time. However, numbers appear to have increased since, and Portree Loch remains a favoured spot with up to 50 birds during the 2003-04 winter. There was a max. count of 35 at Loch Ainort on 28.12.2003. Birds are also seen regularly at Broadford Bay in late summer and autumn and numbers can be high with 69 on 22.10.08 and 60 at nearby Kyleakin on 17.1.2007.

COMMON GULL   *Larus canus*   Faoileag (an t-iasgair diomhain)

Breeding resident. Occurs in large numbers on passage.
Amber list species.

It was described by Macpherson as resident, nesting in the Ascribs, the Colbost Islands and near Broadford. Baxter & Rintoul found it breeding commonly on Skye. Both Collier and Temperley found it breeding on Raasay.

According to the 1968-72 *Atlas* it was widespread, with confirmed breeding from 17 squares although there was a slight contraction in this by 1988-91. Estimates of breeding numbers were obtained in the seabird surveys, with 400 pairs in 1969-70, which reduced to 300 pairs in 1986-87. The species was recorded from the majority of squares during the 1981-83 *Winter Atlas*.

It is difficult to estimate the number of pairs which breed on Skye. Though the seabird surveys provide a baseline, this is a species which also breeds on a number of our inshore lochs and shores and these would not be included. Common Gulls also occur regularly on passage and in winter. However, numbers are not significant, with counts of c200 frequent during WeBS counts in Broadford Bay.

LESSER BLACK-BACKED GULL   *Larus fuscus*   Farspag-bheag

Breeding resident and passage migrant.   **Amber list species.**

Macpherson stated it was resident, nesting on the Ascribs and Waternish Islands. Prideaux said it bred, but not plentifully, on the smaller islands off Skye (in B&R). On Raasay it was found breeding by both Collier and Temperley.

There was confirmed breeding from 11 *Atlas* squares between 1968-72. A similar distribution occurred in 1988-91. During the seabird surveys there was an estimate of 340 breeding pairs in 1986-87, a significant increase from 47 pairs in 1969-70. However, the figure was back to 41 pairs in Seabird 2000. There were winter records from 15 sites during the 1981-83 *Winter Atlas*.

This remains a scarce breeding bird on Skye. It occurs more regularly as a passage migrant. It is occasionally recorded in winter with 2 at lower Milovaig on 17.2.2007

HERRING GULL   *Larus argentatus*   Glas-fhaoileag (faoileag-an-sgadain)

Common breeding resident and passage migrant.   Amber list species.

Resident, with 'immense numbers frequenting the western fiords of Skye, breeding for miles along such fine headlands as Waterstein, Dunvegan and Ramasaig'(Macpherson). Collier found hundreds breeding on the west coast of Raasay, apparently still the case in Temperley's time. Baxter & Rintoul found them common in 1930 and it was also the commonest Gull on Raasay.

There was a widespread coastal distribution according to the 1968-72 and 1988-91 *Breeding Atlas* surveys. During the seabird surveys the population for Skye (& Lochalsh) was 2476 breeding pairs, a significant increase from the estimate of 1329 pairs in 1969-70. It is worth noting that the figure declined significantly during Seabird 2000. During the 1981-83 *Winter Atlas* there was a widespread distribution.

It is not known whether there has been any change in breeding status. Many thousands of birds frequent the coasts of Skye during late summer and autumn taking advantage of rich feeding offshore and in the sea lochs. In their August 1986 survey of north-west Scotland, Burton *et al.* found the largest concentration of this species in the Inner Sound, north of Kyle of Lochalsh. Many of these birds are on passage and a recent count of 3000 at Strathaird Point on 23.9.2003 is a further indication of the numbers involved. It is suspected that numbers tail off during the winter but there are normally 1000+ in the vicinity of Portree.

ICELAND GULL   *Larus glaucoides*   Faoileag liath

A winter visitor in small numbers.

According to Gray it was seen or killed every winter on the coast of Skye. Macpherson, however, found it much scarcer, with only two definite records in 1882 and 1883. In Baxter & Rintoul, Prideaux suggested it was occasional at Portree.

There were singles recorded in the *SBR* on 10.11.1978 (no location) and Portree between 1.1-15.5.1979. B. Philp recorded single birds in successive winters at Portree Bay between 1979 and 1982. It was recorded in 3 squares during the 1981-83 *Winter Atlas*. There was a report of 3 at Portree on 13.2.1984.

Though this is a species whose numbers vary each winter, it is probably regularly overlooked. In 2000, singles were recorded at Camasunary on 23.1 and at Loch Ainort on 26.2. In 2001 it was again recorded at Loch Ainort on 9.3.2001 and at Elgol where there was 1 on 28.3, 2 on 29.3 and 3 on 31.3, feeding on what appeared to be Herring fry. It has been recorded annually in the last few winters. A bird showing many characteristics of Kumlien's Gull was at Broadford on 30.12.2007 (M Benson).

GLAUCOUS GULL   *Larus hyperboreus*   Faoileag-mhòr (muir-mhaighstir)

A winter visitor in small numbers.

Macpherson regarded it as a rare winter visitor, and certainly at that time most met an untimely fate by being shot. This was certainly the case for a number of specimens found between 1885 and 1894. The first record seems to be of a bird shot on the west coast of Skye in 1875. According to Prideaux, in Baxter & Rintoul, there was a very tame adult in Portree Harbour in the summer of 1944.

There were further records from Kyleakin on 27 and 30.4.1969. The species was recorded in 3 squares during the 1981-83 *Winter Atlas*.

More recently a single was recorded at Camastianavaig on 5.2.1988 and an immature at Portnalong in mid August, 199 8. Again, this is a species which is probably regularly overlooked, though it has been recorded in the last few winters.

GREAT BLACK-BACKED GULL   *Larus marinus*   Farspag

Breeding resident and passage migrant.

Macpherson regarded it as resident and breeding on Eilean Isay but provided no data from elsewhere. In Baxter & Rintoul, Prideaux is quoted as suggesting it was increasing. It apparently only nested in small numbers on Raasay.

During the 1968-72 *Atlas* there was confirmed breeding from 22 squares, reflecting a widespread coastal distribution. There was probably a slight increase in 1988-91. The seabird surveys estimated the population for Skye (& Lochalsh) as 368 pairs in 1985-87, a significant increase from the 214 pairs estimated in 1969-70. Seabird 2000 however suggested 151 pairs. It was present in most squares during the 1981-83 *Winter Atlas*.

Like most Gull species, there seems to be very little data available. There are certainly significant movements of this species through Skye in late summer/ autumn and 1000+ in Lochs Slapin/Eishort on 23.9.2003 is an example of this. A winter count of 330 at Loch Ainort on 13.1.2005 is unusual.

BLACK-LEGGED KITTIWAKE   *Rissa tridactyla*   Ruideag (faireag)

Breeds. Large numbers occur on spring and autumn passage.
Amber list species.

According to Macpherson it was resident, numbers nesting at a large station at Greshornish, others near Waternish, and many more at Neist. Collier found only a few pairs breeding on Raasay but they were not there in Temperley's time. Seton Gordon and Prideaux also reported a small number of colonies.

Breeding was confirmed from 4 Atlas squares in 1968-72 and from 6 in 1988-91, reflecting the general expansion of this species throughout the UK. During Operation Seafarer in 1969-70 there were an estimated 883 pairs for Skye. This may well have been an underestimate as the population was thought to be 2086 pairs in the 1985-87 survey. However the estimate was reduced to 1309 pairs in Seabird 2000. It was well distributed, though mostly in small numbers during the 1981-83 *Winter Atlas*, with records from 19 squares. However, breeding numbers have declined in recent years.

Large movements of Kittiwakes occur offshore in several areas of Skye including the Inner Sound off Raasay, in outer Loch Slapin, and off the north-west coast at Neist Point. The size of these movements is such that breeding birds and juveniles from further afield in Scotland are involved. For example 1400 per hour were recorded heading south at Neist Point on 3.11.1978 (*SBR*). There is also a record of 1500 at Loch Snizort on 5.9.1988 (*HBR*). In the survey of north-west Scotland in August 1986, Burton *et al.* found a major concentration in the north of Skye.

More recent counts include 500 in the Sound of Raasay on 30.10.2000, 2000 off Broadford Bay on 27.10.01, 2000 off Strathaird Point on 18.10.02 and 2000 on Lochs Slapin/Eishort on 23.9.2003. It is probably inaccurate to describe these flocks as passage flocks as many remain in our sea lochs through late summer and autumn, finally dispersing southwards towards the end of October. The importance of the rich feeding resources off the Skye coast was identified during the 1986 Seabirds at Sea survey but requires further assessment. An example was an estimated 10,000 birds around the Ascribs on 2.11.2002 following bad weather at sea. Spring passage flocks are less obvious but 700 at Loch Slapin on 9.3.2001 and 500 there on 8.5.2003, are examples. There were also 500 at Camas Mór on 20.6.2003. A count of 2000 in outer Loch Bracadale on 16.4.2003 was exceptional, but may reflect a significant spring passage which largely passes unnoticed.

IVORY GULL   *Pagophila eburnea*

Scarce winter visitor – historical record only.

According to Harvie Brown in *The Fauna* an example was sent by Mr Ross of the Broadford Hotel for identification about 6.2.1901 (*Annals of Scot. Nat. History*).

SANDWICH TERN   *Sterna sandvicensis*   Steàrnan mòr

A regular passage migrant in small numbers.   **Amber list species.**

Macpherson in *The Fauna* cites records from the spring of 1900 at Greshornish and refers to other spring records from Loch Pooltiel.

There is a single square record during the 1968-72 *Breeding Atlas*, but it should be noted that this species has never been known to breed on Skye.

Single birds were reported from Loch Scavaig on 12.6.1980 and Loch Brittle on 1.4.1998. With increased observations, particularly during the last few years, there have been regular records from the Broadford area including 5 at Ashaig 25.8.2001, 3 at Ardnish on 16.4.2003, 3 at Ashaig on 15.6.2003, a single at Strathaird Point on 13.8.2003 and 4 at Waterloo, Broadford, on 15.8.2004. Recent evidence would certainly point to regular annual occurrences of the species, albeit in small numbers. A count of 25 in Broadford Bay on 23.8.2006 was exceptional.

COMMON TERN   *Sterna hirundo*   Stèarnan (falbhag)

Breeds in small numbers and occurs on passage.

Macpherson stated it was a summer visitor nesting on islands off both the south of Skye and the north-west. It is suggested by Seton Gordon and R.C. Prideaux in *The Birds of Scotland* that the species does not nest on the mainland of Skye but, regrettably, little is said about the offshore islands. Temperley found a small colony on an islet on Raasay in 1937 where they had apparently bred for some time, probably the same birds referred to earlier by Collier.

Breeding was confirmed from 9 *Atlas* squares between 1968-72 and had slightly declined by 1988-91. Church and Lodge recorded breeding on Raasay at Oskaig and on Holomon Island in 1982. Seabird surveys have revealed results similar to the *Atlas*. There was an estimate of 200 pairs in 1969-70 which appeared to have significantly reduced to 40+ pairs by 1985-87, similar totals to those found in Seabird 2000 surveys.

Unfortunately there is an absence of data on the current breeding status although there was a count of 50 pairs at Gairbh Eilean, Dunvegan, on 25.6.2007.

ARCTIC TERN   *Sterna paradisaea*   Stèarnan

Breeds in small numbers and occurs on passage.   Amber list species.

Macpherson found it the predominant species in the Ascribs and also breeding elsewhere. Collier found it breeding on Raasay where it was very common. Temperley visited several sites on Raasay during 1936/37, all of which had previously been occupied, but found none. Baxter & Rintoul certainly regard it as the species which predominates on the west coast and in the Hebrides, and Seton Gordon had stated that they still nested on Skye, but apparently in fluctuating numbers.

Breeding was confirmed from 11 *Atlas* squares during the 1968-72 *Atlas*, and although the distribution had changed by 1988-91, the overall status remained much the same. In 1982 Church and Lodge estimated 100+ pairs bred on Fladday. In the seabird surveys there was an estimate of 220 pairs in 1969/70 and this had risen significantly to 1216 pairs in 1985-87. Unfortunately during the Seabird 2000 surveys the estimates had crashed to 209 pairs. There was an estimated 50-70 pairs at Lampay, Claigan, Dunvegan on 24.6.2007

Birds occur on passage though not in significant numbers. There was a late bird on 18.10.1978 though no location is given (*SBR*). More recently there was a late bird at Strathaird Point on 6.10.2003. There is little information on current status, and the only recent counts of note were 200 at Staffin on 12.6.1999 and 112 at Ullinish on 17.6.2003.

LITTLE TERN   *Sterna albifrons*   Stèarnan bheag

Rare passage migrant.   **Amber list species.**

The first record for Skye, presumably a passage bird, was recorded during the 1968-72 *Breeding Atlas*. Single birds were also recorded in the Skye area during the Seabird Surveys of 1969/70 and 1985-87. Probably the significance of these records was lost to the observers as no details are to hand. More recently there are records from Loch Treaslane in 2001 and 2002 and a party of 3 birds was recorded at Ardnish, Broadford, on 21.6.2002.

COMMON GUILLEMOT   *Uria aalge*   Gearradh breac (langaidh)

Breeding resident and passage migrant.   **Amber list species.**

According to Macpherson it was a summer visitor arriving at the beginning of April, and although he mentions it breeding at Lowergill, on the basis of the few records provided, it would appear to have been quite scarce. The birds did not breed on Raasay, but Collier saw large numbers offshore. Prideaux found them on Fladda-chùain but elsewhere they were uncommon (in B&R).

The species was confirmed breeding from 5 squares during the 1968-72 *Atlas* and this had increased to 9 by 1988-91 suggesting some population expansion. All the sites are in the north and west of the island. This is a difficult species to census accurately, but there was a significant increase in site occupancy from the 1969/70 survey when there were 364 occupied sites, to 1985-87 when this had increased substantially to 2290. Over this period the population increased in north-west Scotland by 141%. This increase continued and Seabird 2000 estimated the population at 6470. However, there has been a significant decrease since.

The coastal survey conducted by Ellis in the winter of 1978/79 recorded extremely low numbers, certainly significantly less than can be found to-day. During the 1981-83 *Winter Atlas*, Guillemots were recorded in 14 squares, the largest concentrations being on the sheltered east coast.

There is certainly evidence that large concentrations can occur in late summer and autumn, off the north of Skye, in the Inner Sound and off Pabay. During a ship-based survey of north-west Scotland in August 1986 the highest concentrations of adults and their chicks was in the Little Minch to the north-west of Skye (Burton *et al.* 1987). On the south-west of the island, Lochs Scavaig, Slapin and Eishort can also hold large numbers and it is suspected similar numbers occur in the Sound of Sleat. Many birds are accompanied by young. It also appears that adult birds seen in August/September may be in moult suggesting that birds from colonies further afield, including Eigg, Canna, the Shiants and probably Handa, may exploit fishing in the rich coastal waters of Skye at this time. There is further evidence from the Seabirds at Sea survey that birds from the north-west of Scotland disperse through the Minches into the Sea of Hebrides, rather than to the north and east as had previously been assumed. These flocks number many thousands and peak during August/September, then steadily reduce during October and early November when numbers tail off for the winter.

An example of late summer counts is 1000 at Strathaird Point on 7.9.02. However this is thought to be an underestimate, with count rates of 700 per hour west out of Loch Slapin on 10.10.2003 and similar volumes on 3.11.2003, though numbers declined rapidly later in the month. Winter counts include 200 at Loch Ainort on 26.2.2000.

During late summer 2004 a large Auk 'wreck' occurred off the north-west coast of Scotland (R. Swann pers. comm). This coincided with a period of extremely unsettled weather following which a large number of Guillemots were washed up dead on the Skye coast. On analysis it was found that the birds had died of starvation, an apparent shortage of food coinciding with the bad weather. As a result of surveys along part of the Skye coast over 400 carcases were found but it is suspected that the true number of casualties ran into thousands. Ringed birds recovered on Skye were mainly from the nearby colonies on Canna. A number of birds were also in heavy moult, lending support to the discussion in the previous paragraphs.

RAZORBILL   *Alca torda*   Coltraiche (dui-eunach)

Breeding resident and passage migrant.   **Amber list species.**

Macpherson regarded the species as a summer visitant, breeding on the Ascribs, with apparently 'great numbers breeding on the ledges from Lowergill to Ramasaig'. Collier saw 'thousands' passing Raasay on migration in autumn and spring but they did not breed. Baxter & Rintoul did not elaborate further other than to say that in 1946 Prideaux had found them on Fladda-chùain but that they were uncommon elsewhere.

There was confirmed breeding from 7 *Atlas* squares between 1968-72 and this had slightly increased by 1988-91. All the colonies are in the north and west of Skye and during the seabird surveys of 1985-87 it was estimated that 844 sites were occupied. This was reduced to 623 pairs during Seabird 2000. However, similar to other Scottish colonies, there has been a significant recent decline.

During the 1978/79 winter survey the largest concentrations were on the sheltered east coast between Loch na Cairidh and Portree, with a max. of 400+ for the whole of the Skye coast. The species was recorded from 15 squares during the 1981-83 *Winter Atlas*.

Looking at the historical record it might appear that Razorbills outnumbered Guillemots on Skye. Whilst breeding numbers might be roughly similar, it is certainly not the case during late summer when many are present in the Skye sea lochs. Many adults are in moult and many are accompanied by juveniles. However, though numbers are significantly below that of Guillemots, the coastal waters of Skye are extremely important in late summer and autumn as identified by Burton *et al.* (1986) and the Seabirds at Sea survey.

BLACK GUILLEMOT   *Cepphus grylle arcticus*   Calltag (gearradh glas)

Common breeding resident.   **Amber list species.**

According to Gray there were breeding places on the Ascribs and in similar groups of rocks on the west coast of Skye. This was confirmed by Macpherson who found it breeding in large numbers in the Ascribs, with small colonies elsewhere. It was also regarded as resident with a few birds wintering. Baxter & Rintoul found it common on Skye in 1930. It was found breeding numerously on Raasay in 1937/38 by Temperley, a similar status to that found by Collier earlier.

During the 1968-72 *Atlas* there was either confirmed or probable breeding in 20 squares and there was some improvement in this during 1988-91. Operation Seafarer estimated 180 pairs but this was regarded as a huge underestimate by A. Currie. This is regarded as one of the most difficult species to survey as it breeds at low density and nest sites are hidden in crevices and under boulders. It is therefore difficult to estimate breeding pairs and in present seabird surveys, counts are made of birds on the sea near the breeding sites. In April 1987 a total of 2967 birds were recorded on Skye, the biggest concentration being off the island of Wiay with 129 birds. In Seabird 2000 the count declined to 2672. Nonetheless with an overall Scottish count of over 37,000 birds, Skye is extremely important for this species.

There were comprehensive records from the 1981-83 *Winter Atlas*, the species being recorded in every coastal square, with the largest concentrations in the east side. This confirmed earlier work by Ellis in the winter survey of 1978/79 when there was a suggested total for Skye in February/March of

209, thought to be a significant underestimate. However, birds are normally well scattered along the coast in winter and counts of 50 off Moll on 26.9.2001 and at Ardnish, Broadford, on 2.1.2004 were unusual. Birds start to lose their winter plumage in January and by early spring many are back in breeding territories, 20+ pairs near Elgol on 8.3.2003 being an example.

LITTLE AUK   *Alle alle*   Colcach bheag (falcag)

Regular winter visitor in small numbers.

Its status was that of a rare winter visitant according to Macpherson, occasionally seen off the Ascribs and a number of specimens had been taken. Small numbers were seen by Collier on Raasay in winter. Baxter & Rintoul simply state that it occurs on Skye. On 16.1.1937 J. W. Campbell reported many hundreds flying northwest off the north coast of Skye (*SN*).

There was only a single record from Loch Slapin during the 1981-83 *Winter Atlas*.

Between 1976 and 1996 there were only a handful of records, from Kilmaluag, Staffin, Loch Brittle, Kylerhea and Broadford Bay. Occasionally blown inland there were 5 at Aird, Sleat, on 10.2.1988. Most records are between December-March. During the last few years there have been an increasing number of records, particularly in the Broadford Bay area. This confirms observations made in the Lochalsh area by Brian Neath, which suggest the species is much more regular in winter than previously considered. There have also been recent records from the Sound of Sleat, Loch Slapin, Portree Loch and Loch Snizort. However, it should be emphasised that the overall numbers involved are small, the best count being 15 at Kylerhea on 4.1.2002.

ATLANTIC PUFFIN   *Fratercula arctica*   Fachach (coltrachan)

Breeds in small numbers on offshore islands.   Amber list species.

Martin Martin (1697) said that 'Coulternebs' were very numerous on Fladda-chùain off Skye and the species is mentioned in the *Old Statistical Account* for the same location. Writing of the same site in 1841, Wilson said the birds were so numerous they covered the rocks and the neighbouring cliffs. 'Considerable numbers incubate on the Ascribs and other rocky islets off the coast of Skye' (Gray). Macpherson also found it 'breeding in immense numbers in the Ascribs' and also recorded it in November at Loch Pooltiel, commenting that this was 'a curious fact for those who perversely hold that these birds leave our coast in winter'. Baxter & Rintoul quote Seton Gordon, who stated that they still bred on the Ascribs as well as on An t-Iasgair. Puffins have never been known to breed on Raasay but were seen offshore by Collier.

During the 1968-72 *Atlas* there was confirmed breeding in 4 squares and in 1988-91 there was evidence of breeding in 5 squares. Sites are restricted to islands off the north of Skye, the largest colony of which is Fladda-chùain. However, numbers are relatively small with 465 pairs in 1969/70, which had increased to 616 pairs in 1985-87. Unfortunately the population had apparently declined to 110 pairs during the Seabird 2000 survey. The Seabirds at Sea survey in 1986 highlighted the importance of the sea off the north of Skye for Puffins, especially in August, prior to the birds' post breeding dispersal.

Despite the comment by Macpherson above, it was not recorded during the 1981-83 *Winter Atlas* illustrating the largely pelagic nature of the species in winter. Following bad weather at sea many birds were seen in the Sound of Raasay on 8.11.2002 (*HBR*). There is also a report of a single bird at Dunvegan Pier on 7.1.2003, which is unusual. Normally, birds move back to breeding teritories in March/April.

PALLAS'S SANDGROUSE *Syrrhaptes paradoxus*

Accidental visitor – historical records only.

Macpherson cites two separate reports which probably refer to the same group of birds, 14 being seen at Duntulm on 28.5.1888, and 8 near the Ascribs on 12.6 of the same year. One of the birds from the Duntulm group was shot and 'winged', and kept in captivity for over a year before it 'succumbed to terriers'. (This species has a tendency to irrupt and in May 1888 there was a spectacular invasion estimated to number 1500-2000 across Scotland, and birds subsequently bred. Apparently the fate of the above bird was fairly typical and at the time they were terribly persecuted (B&R).)

ROCK PIGEON *Columba livia* Calman creige (calman mara)

Breeding resident.

The *Old Statistical Account* in 1795 has a record of Doves breeding in the rocks of Strath. MacGillivray suggested Skye was one of the best places to study the species. Macpherson found it common and resident 'though perhaps decreasing owing to cattle being fed more indoors in winter than formerly'. Collier found it in the caves on the coast of Raasay. Baxter & Rintoul found them common on Skye in 1930 and quoted Seton Gordon, who was aware of a small inland breeding colony.

During the 1968-72 *Atlas* there was confirmed breeding in 13 squares, most, surprisingly, in the north of the island and there was seemingly some decline by 1988-91. Populations continue to be contaminated by birds showing feral pigeon characteristics. It was recorded in small numbers in 17 squares during the 1981-83 *Winter Atlas*.

Although there are birds in the population which are not pure, a significant proportion of Skye birds exhibit general plumage and behavioural characteristics of typically wild examples of the species. Changes in crofting practices may have affected food availability, especially in winter when it is not uncommon to see birds near bird tables. Winter counts include 29 at Glen Brittle on 13.12.1978 (*SBR*), 30 at Staffin on 9.2.1979, 40 at Brogaig on 17.9.1999, 28 at Breakish on 28.2.02, and counts of 35 at Elgol on 22.10.2003 and Camastianavaig on 26.10.2003. Birds will regularly use feeding stations and up to 75 were recorded at Faoilean, Strathaird, in autumn 2004.

COMMON WOOD PIGEON *Columba palumbus* Calman coille (guragag)

Breeding resident.

According to Gray it was found on Skye. Macpherson stated it was resident but on the basis of the limited reports it would seem to have been scarce. However, this was certainly not the case on Raasay where Collier found it breeding and flocks of 60-80 present in winter. There was a suggestion it may have been spreading in the Highlands generally and Baxter & Rintoul elaborate on this. They found a pair at Uig in June 1910 and by 1930 found small numbers breeding. Temperley found it a plentiful resident around Raasay House in 1936/37.

It was confirmed as 'breeding', or 'probably bred' in 22 *Atlas* squares in 1968-72 but by 1988-91 there was an apparent decline, especially in the north of the island. The distribution during the 1981-83 *Winter Atlas* was, surprisingly, restricted to 11 squares.

The extensive afforestation on the island during the last 20 years should have helped this species. Whilst it appears to have a wide distribution, there are no reports of flocks of any size. Availability of food during the winter months may be a factor.

EURASIAN COLLARED DOVE   *Streptopelia decaocto*

Breeding resident.

The speedy colonisation of Britain since 1955 by this species is one of the most remarkable ornithological events of the 20th century. The first record for Scotland was in 1957 and the first record for Skye was thought to have been in 1963 (Thom).

It was confirmed or probably bred in 13 *Atlas* squares in 1968-72. However, by 1988-91, if anything, there had been a marginal contraction in range. The species was recorded in only 9 squares during the 1981-83 *Winter Atlas*.

It is not thought that there has been any change in the status of this species, but surprisingly little data is available.

EUROPEAN TURTLE DOVE   *Streptopelia turtur*   Turtar (colgan)

Rare migrant.   **Red list species.**

Macpherson admits that he questioned previous records of this species in Skye but put the matter beyond doubt when he shot (for identification!) an adult male at Hamara, Glendale, in June 1886. One was observed at Colbost the following year. According to Baxter & Rintoul there was also a record for Raasay.

The species was recorded in Sleat on 18.5.1995. There was a further record at Glen Hinnisdal on 28.5.1996. More recently there is a report from Dunvegan on 24.-25.5.2002 and a reliable report from Kyleakin in June of the same year. There was a bird at Isle Ornsay for 3 days from 18.6.2003. There have been several records since including a spring and autumn record in 2008.

COMMON CUCKOO   *Cuculus canorus*   Cubhag

Common summer visitor.   **Amber list species.**

Macpherson suggests it is a summer visitant (or perhaps an irritant, according to his later description) 'most obstreperous in the gloaming, when the challenge of the males to the 'whittling' females, awakes the remonstrances of the sleepy thrushes'. Collier found it plentiful on Raasay where it favoured Meadow Pipits' nests. It was found by Baxter & Rintoul to be a common summer visitor to Skye and Raasay.

During the 1968-72 and 1988-71 *Atlas* it was recorded in most squares.

This species continues to be an extremely common summer visitor. Historically it arrived towards the end of April, but there has been a tendency over recent years for the first calls to be heard in mid-April. Its departure in late summer is as silent as its arrival is noisy.

BARN OWL   *Tyto alba*   Comhachag bhàn (sgreuchag oidhche)

Breeding resident in small numbers.   **Amber list species.**

It is described in *The Fauna* as resident with records, including breeding, from various parts of Skye. Collier recorded it as an occasional visitor to Raasay. Baxter & Rintoul record that Seton Gordon had a pair nesting in a cleft of rock near his home. It was recorded in Sleat in 1937.

During the 1968-72 *Atlas* it probably bred in 3 squares and was recorded in several others. By 1988-91 it certainly appeared that this limited range had contracted in line with a significant decline elsewhere in the country. According to Andrew Currie a few pairs breed on Skye and possible breeding was recorded in Raasay Forest in 1982. It was recorded in 3 squares during the 1981-83 *Winter Atlas*.

Apparently a number of birds have been released on Skye in a captive breeding programme but no details are available. It is difficult to estimate the size of the population but a number of pairs still nest, all the known sites being in clefts in natural rock. For example in 2004 at least 2 young fledged from a remote site near the head of Loch Scavaig. Young Barn Owls disperse over a large area and the recovery of a bird near Uig, which had been ringed in a nest on Arran, is extremely interesting (*Migration Atlas*) and may indicate natural recruitment to the population.

SNOWY OWL   *Bubo scandiacus*   Comhachag gheal (comhachag mhòr)

Very rare winter visitor – mostly historical records.

Gray suggested that this species was a regular spring visitant to the Outer Hebrides in the 19th century and 'has been met with on Skye in several instances'. Macpherson refers to a further occurrence in the north of Skye later in the 19th century.

Sillar & Meyler, writing in 1973, suggested that the species was recorded 'some years ago' and that the stuffed specimen held by Colonel 'Jock' Macdonald at that time was believed to have been shot on the island.

There have been no recent records.

TAWNY OWL   *Strix aluco*   Comhachag dhonn (bodach-oidhche)

Breeding resident.

A common resident in all the wooded districts according to *The Fauna* but there is no specific reference to Skye – neither had Gray earlier. However, in his 1889 note to *The Zoologist*, Macpherson stated that the species had been 'obtained in several quarters'. Collier proved successful breeding on Raasay in 1901. Perry reported it in the birch wood above Loch na Béiste in the late 1930s and around the same time, Temperley found a few pairs breeding on Raasay. It was also breeding in Sleat in 1937.

It was confirmed or probably bred in 14 *Atlas* squares in 1968-72 but a slight decline was recorded in 1988-91. Surprisingly it was recorded in only 6 squares during the 1981-83 *Winter Atlas*. Thom suggested that the apparent increase in breeding records for Skye and Raasay during the preceeding 30-40 years was due to afforestation. It certainly appeared to have significantly increased throughout the 20th century.

The Tawny Owl appears to be widely distributed as a breeding resident.

LONG-EARED OWL   *Asio otus*   Comhachag adharcaiche (mulchan)

Rare breeding resident.

Though 'less common', Gray suggested it breeds in Skye in limited numbers, and this is supported by Macpherson who regarded it as a resident and provided several examples of breeding. In *Birds of Scotland* Seton Gordon had recorded it on Skye but had never found a nest, whilst Collier said it occasionally bred on Raasay. Perry recorded it above Loch na Béiste.

There were no records during the 1968-72 or 1988-91 *Atlas* surveys. B. Philp recorded a pair breeding at Skirinish in 1980. Neither was there a record during the 1981-83 *Winter Atlas* survey. Andrew Currie is quoted by Thom as suggesting that several pairs may be present on Skye.

The only recent records include young calling from a nest at Linicro 1.-2.6.1995, and 3 young blown from a nest at Elgol on 1.6.1996 and a pair near Uig on 7.8.2007. The species may be regularly overlooked.

SHORT-EARED OWL   *Asio flammeus*   Comhachag chluasach

Rare breeding resident.   **Amber list species.**

Gray suggests it was resident all the year round on Skye and further evidence is provided by Macpherson in *The Fauna*, though none of breeding. According to Collier it had bred on Raasay prior to his time. Surprisingly, there were no records from Baxter & Rintoul.

At the time of the 1968-72 *Atlas* the position was improved with confirmed or probable breeding in 10 squares. Reed *et al.* suggested that the species had benefited from young plantations on Skye though there appeared to have been a decline in 1988-91. It was recorded in 5 squares during the 1981-83 *Winter Atlas*. Thom suggested that breeding occurred regularly on Skye and again suggested that numbers were increasing as a result of afforestation.

This is a species whose numbers fluctuate dramatically according to the vole population. Sightings of individual birds are now scarce and worthy of note. Pairs successfully bred in 2007 and 2008 but the overall population is small.

EUROPEAN NIGHTJAR   *Caprimulgus europaeus*   Sgraicheag oidche

Has bred – historical records only.   **Red list species.**

Gray suggested the species was 'generally distributed' on Skye and though Macpherson suggested it was a 'summer visitant' to the south of Skye he provided no evidence to support this. Collier considered it a sparse but annual visitor to Raasay (1896-1902). Temperley did not see it on Raasay. Baxter &

Rintoul provided no further evidence.

It has not been possible to find a record for Skye or Raasay since the turn of the 20th century. This is a species which at one time was widespread throughout Scotland but was declining by the 1930s. By the 1960s it was becoming extremely scarce and by 1981 when a national survey was conducted, it was only recorded at 25 sites in Scotland (Thom 1986). This general decline has continued and although there were apparently reports of churring birds in 1999 and 2004, these remain unconfirmed. A dead bird was found near Kylerhea on 3.8.2005.

COMMON SWIFT   *Apus apus*   Gobhlan dubh (ainleag dhubh)

No recent breeding records. Regular passage migrant.

According to Gray the species was rare on the Inner Hebrides and later, Macpherson only regarded it as a 'casual visitant' and had no knowledge of birds breeding. A few were seen on Raasay every year but they did not breed according to Collier. In 1936/37 Temperley saw none on Raasay. Writing in 1931 Seton Gordon stated categorically that the species did not nest on Skye and it was surprising that Baxter & Rintoul provided no record from Skye.

Though it was recorded at several sites during the 1968-72 and 1988-91 *Atlas* surveys, breeding was not confirmed. It was thought that many of these birds were merely passing through. There remains no evidence of breeding on Skye, supporting Thom's premise that on the west coast there are few breeding birds north of Fort William.

Records of 9 at Armadale on 25.7.1983 and 6 at Portree on 22.5.1996 are unusual. Though records are annual, numbers are small. For example in 2003 there were 4 records in May and June. Unprecedented numbers were recorded between 10.-12.8.2004 when there were reports of c200 at Harrapool, 10 at Carbost and 50 at Glen Brittle. There is no explanation for this unusual influx.

ALPINE SWIFT   *Apus melba*

Extremely rare vagrant.

There is a record from Ardtreck Point, Portnalong, on 23.7.1979 (*SB* No.10).

COMMON KINGFISHER   *Alcedo atthis*   Biorra crùidein (biorra an iasgair)

A scarce vagrant. No known breeding record.   **Amber list species.**

Gray suggested the species had been found on Skye in the 19th century and Macpherson later refers to observations at Lynedale in the summer of 1878.

There is an apparently reliable report of a bird seen on Skye on 14.9.1934 (*SN* 1935) but with no details of location. A bird was seen in Glen Brittle between 6.-9.9.1984 (K. Crane & K. Nellist) and a bird was present in the Sconser area around the same time (A.Currie). More recently a bird was present in the Kinloch/Isle Ornsay area in September/October 2002, and a bird was back in the same area on 23.10.2004 (Roger & Pat Cottis). There was also a record at Drynoch on 2.9.2006.

EUROPEAN BEE-EATER   *Merops apiaster*

A scarce vagrant.

The first record for Skye was a bird at Linicro on 6.-7.6.1993 (*HBR*), and another was seen in Elgol on 17.5.2008 (Mathew Kirk).

HOOPOE   *Upupa epops*

A scarce vagrant.

Macpherson refers to an article in *The Field* which reported that in the middle of October, 1880, a bird was shot in the Sconser Deer Forest. Later, *The Scotsman* reported there was one at Waternish on 27.4.1909. Thom referred to recent records from Skye, which probably included reports from Caroy and Dunvegan in April/May 1976 and a single on Raasay on 25.4.1984. A bird was seen at Galtrigill, Glendale, on 14.9.1995, presumably the same bird which had moved to Ullinish on 16.9.1995. The most recent records were spring birds at Borve between 21-23.4.2003 and at Flodigarry/Kilmaluag on 23.4.2008. A bird was also on Raasay for several days in August 2006.

WRYNECK   *Jynx torquilla*

Very scarce vagrant.

The only report which can be traced for Skye is of a single bird, presumably a migrant, in the Glendale area on 3.9.2000 (*HBR*).

GREAT SPOTTED WOODPECKER   *Dendrocopos major*   Snagair daraich
(lair fligh)

A rare breeding resident, probably expanding its range.

Although there is no record in *The Fauna*, writing in *The Zoologist* in 1889, Macpherson spoke of a bird shot at Edinbane in October 1886 and which he later examined. Macpherson claimed this was a 'first' for the Hebrides. Baxter & Rintoul refer to a record from Skye but implied that this was continental immigration, and unfortunately, because no date was provided, it is not known whether this was the earlier record by Macpherson. The species steadily re-colonised Scotland during the first half of the 20th century but it has yet to be established when it first reached Skye. Thom is unable to provide a date, suggesting it was post 1953.

By the time of the 1968-72 *Atlas* breeding was probable in 5 squares, 4 of which were on Sleat. It was recorded on Raasay by Church and Lodge in 1982. It was subsequently recorded in 2 squares during the 1981-83 *Winter Atlas*. It was recorded at Dunvegan Castle on 6.4.1985. Surprisingly, however, the species appeared to have declined by 1988-91 when it was recorded in only 1 square.

Though Great Spotted Woodpeckers have been reported from a variety of locations throughout Skye, there is an absence of breeding records away from the core area of colonisation which was Sleat. Given the quality of mixed woodlands in the Sleat peninsula it is understandable that this remains the prime area though the size of the population is difficult to estimate. In the Garden Wildlife Survey of 2003, 6% of gardens in Skye recorded the species, all in the south of the island. Records from further north, as at Kensaleyre and Greshornish, are unusual.

SKYLARK   *Alauda arvensis*   Uiseag (fosgag Moire)

Breeds commonly – a few birds winter. Occurs on passage.
Red list species.

Although described by Macpherson as a summer visitant, nesting chiefly on the verge of arable land, there was other evidence in *The Fauna* that some remained through the winter. Collier found a few pairs nesting on Raasay. According to Seton Gordon in Baxter & Rintoul there was a great immigration of larks to Skye in October, arriving from the north-east, and he considers that most of the wintering birds are immigrants.

The species probably bred in every square during the 1968-72 and 1988-91 *Atlas* surveys. Most birds disperse in winter but it was recorded in 7 squares during the 1981-83 *Winter Atlas*, all of which were in the north of the island. Given Seton Gordon's earlier remarks, 60 at Trumpan, Waternish, on 22.11.1978 was an interesting observation.

This is a species which is under threat elsewhere hence its current red list status. There is little evidence that breeding numbers are declining on Skye. It certainly appears, however, that the majority of birds are absent in winter, returning migrants starting to appear in February.

HORNED (SHORE) LARK *Eremophila alpestris* Uiseag dhubh

Extremely scarce winter visitor.

Though Thom refers to a record for Skye, obviously prior to 1986, further details have not been established.

SAND MARTIN *Riparia riparia* Gobhlan-gainmhich (fallach)

Breeds in small numbers and occurs on passage. Amber list species.

Several records of nesting are referred to in *The Fauna* by Macpherson, all at the end of the 19th century. Collier had a few on Raasay in the spring but they did not breed. Baxter & Rintoul saw a few in 1910 and 1930.

It was confirmed as breeding in only 5 squares during the 1968-72 *Atlas* and there was apparently some decline by 1988-91. According to Thom the species bred regularly but in small numbers on Skye.

There are only a few colonies on Skye and all of these are on a small scale.

BARN SWALLOW *Hirundo rustica* Gobhlan gaoithe (ainleag)

Breeds. Common summer visitor. **Amber list species.**

Though described as a summer visitant in *The Fauna*, there were only a few known records of breeding. Captain MacDonald of Waternish, writing in 1886, suggested they bred in great numbers in cliffs along the coast but this was never confirmed. Although it had been known to breed on Raasay, it seemed scarce, and only a few pairs were found by Collier. According to Temperley it was absent from Raasay as a breeding bird in 1936/37. Seton Gordon wrote in 1931 that it was absent from much of Skye, and was seldom seen apart from Sleat and parts of Trotternish. Baxter & Rintoul found a few pairs nesting at Broadford, giving the impression was that it was not particularly common. There was certainly a perception that there was an increase during the 1960-70s (A. Currie pers. comm.).

It was confirmed as breeding or probably breeding in 20 squares during the 1968-72 *Atlas* and there was a similar distribution in 1988-91.

Though there is a lack of comparative data, current evidence certainly suggests that the species is much more widespread than previously and this would tend to suggest a steady population expansion during the last 30 years, which has largely passed unnoticed. Birds are slower to settle and nest than on the mainland, but will normally raise 2 broods. There is currently some evidence however of birds arriving earlier and a single at Broadford on 24.3.2003 was exceptional. At the other end of the scale, 3 at Kyleakin on 1.12.2002 was extremely late.

In 2000 a roost was discovered in phragmites beds at Loch Cill Chriosd with a count of 500 birds on 12.8. This has been occupied between late July and September in every year since, with numbers peaking at a similar level. Sand Martins have also used the site.

HOUSE MARTIN   *Delichon urbicum*   Gobhlan taighe

Summer visitor and breeds in small numbers.   Amber list species.

Though Gray said it was common on Skye, it was only described by Macpherson as a summer visitant, but it was difficult to assess in what numbers. Collier observed a few in spring but did not know it to breed on Raasay, a similar position to that found later by Temperley. Baxter & Rintoul found it scarce, only two birds being seen at Portree in 1930 and although it had apparently nested at Kyleakin, it had ceased to do so.

During the 1968-72 *Atlas* it was only confirmed to breed in 4 squares, 3 of which were in the north of the island. It was equally scarce in 1988-91.

Unfortunately it is a species whose nesting habits on buildings sometimes make it unpopular, but it is worth emphasising that this is locally a rare breeding bird. In 2003 it bred at Broadford and young were still being attended in the nest on 5.10. In 2004 at least 3 pairs nested at a house in Torrin where the species had not previously been known. It continues to nest at scattered locations.

TREE PIPIT   *Anthus trivialis*   Riabhag choille

Summer visitor and breeds.   Amber list species.

There is no reference to the species by Macpherson which suggests it had probably been overlooked, as Collier had found a few pairs nesting on the edge of woods on Raasay. In 1930 Baxter & Rintoul found them at Kyleakin, Portree and Dunvegan. Temperley found them in Raasay in the 1930s. In the 1940s Perry found birds in the birch wood at Loch na Béiste.

It was confirmed breeding in 10 squares during the 1968-72 *Atlas* and although there was some evidence of a decrease in 1988-91, this is a species which is easily overlooked.

Unfortunately little is known on the current breeding status of Tree Pipits on Skye, though it continues to be recorded fairly widely.

MEADOW PIPIT   *Anthus pratensis*   Snathag (didig)

Common breeding resident. Passage migrant.   Amber list species.

According to Macpherson it was a summer visitant, the commonest small bird on the hillside in the nesting season. Collier found it distributed over the whole island on Raasay. In September, 1937, Seton Gordon came across a small party of pipits on passage on the rocky summit of Sgurr na Banachdich in the Cuillin presumably birds on the move south: 'the pipits rose into the mist, and sailed daintily and carelessly over a great 1,000-feet precipice'.

A ubiquitous species in Skye, it bred in every *Atlas* square during 1968-72 and 1988-91. Most birds disperse in winter but it was recorded in 20 squares in the 1981-83 *Winter Atlas*, though in small numbers.

The *Migration Atlas* suggests that many birds winter throughout the lowlands of Britain and Ireland into western continental Europe. During the early 1970s many birds were ringed on Pabay by Ted Gerrard. Birds ringed in August and September were subsequently recovered in November in France and Spain. On the west of Scotland visible migration can sometimes be seen, and certainly on Skye it is possible to watch small parties launch themselves nervously over the sea, from promontories such as Strathaird Point and the Point of Sleat. Travelling in small groups it appears they are 'island hopping', moving generally in a southerly direction. Observations on such movements have been noted between late July and late October and obviously involve many thousands of birds.

Some reasonable flocks have been recorded in autumn and 200 at Staffin on 22.9.2001 is a good example. As indicated earlier, small numbers of birds overwinter. Arrival back in the spring is less obvious. Though birds will occupy territories quickly in early spring, flocks can occur after a cold snap and 150 at Strathaird on 28.4.2000 was an example of this.

ROCK PIPIT   *Anthus petrosus*   Gabhagan

Common breeding resident.

Macpherson in *The Fauna* describes it as 'everywhere abundant, both on the coasts of the mainland and on the rocky islands throughout the area.' Collier found it plentiful on the coast of Raasay. Baxter & Rintoul have nothing to add.

It was recorded breeding in virtually every coastal square during the 1968-72 and 1988-91 *Atlas* surveys. During the 1981-83 *Winter Atlas* it was recorded in 22 squares.

Resident birds are mostly territorial throughout the winter but loose feeding flocks can sometimes be found at high tide. For example, on 25.11.2001 counts on three small bays on Loch Slapin near Torrin, aggregated to 34 birds, with a strong possibility that some of these were immigrants. On 19.12.2004 50 were counted on a 1.5 km stretch of coast near Elgol.

WATER PIPIT   *Anthus spinoletta*

Very rare passage migrant.

The only record of this rare vagrant is at Loch Caroy, Harlosh, on the unusual date of 29.6.1992 (*HBR*).

YELLOW WAGTAIL   *Motacilla flava*   Breacan buidhe

Has bred, but no recent records.   **Amber list species.**

Collier suggested that 2 pairs bred on Raasay from 1896 to 1902: 'they came at the end of April or beginning of May, nidification taking place soon after their arrival. The young and old birds left again between the 10th and the middle of September'. This species has not been recorded subsequently and though Raasay may be perceived as somewhat north of their normal range in Scotland. Collier was excellent in the field and there is no reason to doubt his identification, which was subsequently accepted by Thom. There is only one recent report, a single at Dunvegan on 7.8.2008 (A. Stables).

GREY WAGTAIL   *Motacilla cinerea*   Breacan baintighearna
                                            (bricein an uillt)

Breeds commonly. A few birds winter.   **Amber list species.**

According to Gray it was not an uncommon 'winter' visitor to Skye but, surprisingly, there was no record of it breeding. Macpherson correctly described it as a summer visitant, but not numerous. Collier found it common on Raasay: 'every stream has its pair', and also had a few winter records, though Temperley seems to have searched the island diligently in 1936/37 but could not find any. Baxter & Rintoul added little regarding its status.

It was confirmed breeding in 19 squares during the 1968-72 *Atlas* and there was little change in 1988-91. During the 1981-83 *Winter Atlas* it was only recorded in 4 squares. Bearing in mind the remarks regarding Raasay above, it was interesting that Church and Lodge had only a single 'possible' sighting in 1982.

This species is mainly migratory in Skye, and the few which remain during the winter are usually recorded singly and are widely dispersed, a reflection on their territorial behaviour, even in winter. For example during the winter of 2000/01 singles were recorded at 4 separate localities in Strathaird alone. A record of 9 at Armadale on 1.10.1978 is unusual.

In the absence of comparative data it is difficult to comment on the present breeding status.

PIED WAGTAIL   *Motacilla alba yarrellii*   Breac an t-sìl (tachailleag)

Breeds commonly. A few birds winter.

Gray noted in the late 19th century that the Inner Hebrides was deserted by the species in winter. However, it does not seem to have been too common a breeding bird, as Macpherson in *The Fauna* described it as a summer visitant, nesting sporadically in cultivated districts. Collier found it breeding, and though it was a summer visitor he had occasional singles in winter. Baxter & Rintoul had little further to add other than that it bred all over Scotland.

During the 1968-72 and 1988-91 *Atlas* surveys it was breeding in most squares. It would certainly appear that the species was much more widely distributed than the historical record suggested. During the 1981-83 *Winter*

Atlas it was recorded in 8 squares underlying the fact that this species is mostly migratory in Skye. Those birds which do winter are normally found around settlements and habitation where feeding is available.

On a fine evening in late summer groups of Pied Wagtails have been seen at Strathaird Point, heading out to sea on their journey south. For example on 26.8.2001 20 flew south over the sea from Strathaird Point and birds have also been seen moving during daylight hours. Return migration is less obvious, the first birds arriving back in February. A count of 20 at Broadford on 21.3.2003 was thought to comprise returning spring birds.

This is also a species which roosts communally. Loch Cill Chriosd is a favoured locality and 50-100 birds roost in phragmites at the loch edge in late summer

WHITE WAGTAIL   *Motacilla alba alba*   Gocan cìreanach

A regular passage migrant, particularly in late spring.

Only in the latter half of the 19th century was this species differentiated and recognised as a migrant. The first record for Skye appears to be by Baxter & Rintoul at Kyleakin on 20.5.1930. It was also recorded by Henson on Pabay in March, 1956, although this is an extremely early date. When T. Gerrard was ringing on Pabay in the 1970s he regularly caught the species in late summer/autumn.

All the records for Skye are in the last few years and concentrated in the Strathaird area, but this is merely coincidental. Spring arrivals commence in April with peak passage through early May and it is thought that these birds are Icelandic in origin. Counts include 5 at Point of Sleat on 3.5.2001, 6 at Camas Malag, Torrin, on 26.4.2002, 19 there on 5.5.2003 and 6 on 25.4.2004. Returning birds in late summer are less obvious but nonetheless do occur in August and September, albeit in small numbers.

BOHEMIAN WAXWING   *Bombycilla garrulus*   Gocan cìreanach
                                                          (canranach dearg)

Rare but regular winter visitor.

According to Gray a specimen was shot on Skye in 1850, but there were no subsequent records known to either Harvie-Brown or Macpherson.

It was recorded in only a single square during the 1981-83 *Winter Atlas*, but in good 'irruption' years it would be expected to be more widespread. There was such an invasian during 1996 with good numbers reported throughout the island, best counts in late January being 20 at Broadford. There was a further invasion the following winter with 18 at Strathaird on 1.12.1996. Irruptions have occurred during the last few winters which have brought a smattering of records throughout Skye, though birds rarely linger more than a few days.

As the *Migration Atlas* suggests, there is an almost mystical unpredictability about the movement of Waxwings. The birds originate from Scandinavia and Eastern Europe, but even in good years, may not penetrate as far as the west coast. When they do however, a treat is in store and 2004 was such a year. Birds arrived earlier than normal in late October, and there were some huge flocks with 200 at Staffin, 150 at Dunvegan, 100 at Ferindonald in Sleat and at Kensaleyre. Significant flocks were recorded throughout the island in what would certainly appear to have been an unprecedented year. There was a further invasion in early November 2008 with 400+ recorded in Portree.

WHITE-THROATED DIPPER   *Cinclus cinclus*   Gobha uisge
                                                        (gobha dubh an uisge)

Breeding resident.

It was a resident, nesting on all burns according to Macpherson. Collier found 1-2 pairs on every stream on Raasay where later, Temperley found it 'resident' but evidently in small numbers. Although Baxter & Rintoul found several pairs nesting it was difficult to comment on its overall status.

The species was confirmed as breeding in 14 squares during the 1968-72 *Atlas*, though was surprisingly absent from the whole of Sleat. In 1982 Church and Lodge recorded a pair on Raasay but could not confirm breeding. It was not surprising that there was confirmed breeding from Sleat in 1988-91. It was found in 12 squares during the 1981-83 *Winter Atlas*.

Dippers prefer fast flowing, unpolluted streams and rivers, in upland areas, and there is no shortage of such habitat on Skye. It is therefore surprising that the distribution appears to be patchy.

WINTER WREN   *Troglodytes troglodytes*   Dreathan donn (dreòlan)

Common breeding resident.

The Fauna stated it was resident and pretty numerous and Macpherson suggested the bars on the flanks and back are darker in Skye Wrens than in those from southern Britain, and that the bill and feet of the Skye birds appear to be a trifle stronger than their English counterparts! Collier found it common on Raasay. Baxter & Rintoul found the Wren common and Perry found it regularly at 1500-2000 feet.

On the basis of the 1968-72 and 1988-91 *Atlas* surveys it was a ubiquitous breeding species. It was surprisingly absent from a number of squares during the 1981-83 *Winter Atlas*, probably reflecting poor observer coverage.

Other than the above, little seems to be known about this hardy and adaptable species which alone greets us in some pretty dark and inhospitable corners of the island, during short, dreich, winter days.

HEDGE ACCENTOR (DUNNOCK)   *Prunella modularis*   Gealbhonn nam preas (gealbhonn gàraidh)

Common breeding resident.   **Amber list species.**

It was described by Macpherson as 'Resident; thinly distributed occasionally nesting in very lonely situations.' Collier found it on most parts of Raasay. Again Baxter & Rintoul refer to a Hebridean form which was widely distributed in suitable localities, but the separation into such a sub-species has since been abandoned.

It was confirmed breeding in most squares during the 1968-72 *Atlas*. There was apparently some decline during the 1988-91 survey, a factor which was identified throughout the Highlands. In the 1981-83 *Winter Atlas* it was recorded in 14 squares.

The Dunnock can still be found in some pretty remote localities, somewhat at odds with our urban perception of the species. It has also adapted well to breeding in forest plantations.

EUROPEAN ROBIN   *Erithacus rubecula*   Brù-dhearg (ruadhag)

Common breeding resident and winter visitor.

According to Gray it was a common bird on all the Inner Hebrides. Macpherson agreed that it was resident, and 'often to be seen at the roadside, though not nearly so numerous as in England'. Though Collier found it on Raasay it was not numerous. Baxter & Rintoul found it common throughout Skye during the breeding season.

It was confirmed breeding in most squares during the 1968-72 and 1988-91 *Atlas* surveys. Thom suggested that it was scarce or sporadic through most of Skye but there seems to have been little justification for this. During the 1981-83 *Winter Atlas* it was also well distributed.

The Robin remains a common breeding bird and can be found nesting quite remotely. It has also adapted well and can be found breeding widely in coniferous forests of varying ages. There is a major movement of Robins into Scotland from Scandinavia which has been well documented. It would certainly appear that this influx penetrates as far as Skye as there is a noticeable increase in numbers around late autumn. Whether local breeding birds are truly resident remains a mystery, or challenge, in some future ringing project.

BLACK REDSTART   *Phoenicurus ochruros*

A scarce vagrant.   **Amber list species.**

The first record appears to be a single bird at Talisker Bay on 2.1.1995. There was a spring record of an adult male at Ord on 28-29.5.2005 then an immature at Kensaleyre on 18.10.2005. There was also a report from Glendale on 25.10.2007.

COMMON REDSTART   *Phoenicurus phoenicurus*   Ceann-deargan (eàrr-dearg)

Rare summer visitor which breeds in small numbers. Amber list species.

Although Macpherson had no record for Skye, Collier had found 3 pairs nesting in Raasay in 1896 and in subsequent years. Baxter & Rintoul saw a male at Kyleakin in May 1930. The species was later found nesting not far away by Perry at Loch na Béiste where he estimated there were 4 pairs, probably the first confirmed breeding on Skye itself. Mrs Seton Gordon also found a nest at Dunvegan.

During the 1968-72 *Atlas* breeding was confirmed in 3 squares and was probable in 2 others. Richmond (1968) suggested that it bred in hazel scrub near Torrin. Church and Lodge confirmed breeding on Raasay in 1982. There was an apparent decline by the time of the 1988-91 *Atlas* which reflected overall national trends.

A single at Waterstein on 24.9.1986 was likely to be a passage migrant and it is interesting to speculate that in certain favourable conditions in the autumn, more birds might occur. Ted Gerrard certainly caught the species on Pabay when he was ringing there in the 1970s. Otherwise, Redstarts continue to be recorded from a few sites on Skye where there are favourable mature native woodlands.

WHINCHAT   *Saxicola rubetra*   Gocan (fraoichean)

Common summer visitor which breeds.

It was a summer visitant but local according to Macpherson. Collier also found it scarce on Raasay though by Temperley's time it appeared to have increased. However, Baxter & Rintoul saw a good many about Uig in 1910, and in 1930 ' found it common almost everywhere, on the moors, pastures, and sea braes and in the scattered woods of natural birch'. It was well distributed on Raasay and James Fisher found it on Soay in 1942.

At the time of the 1968-72 *Atlas* it bred extensively, being present in most squares and there seemed to be little change by 1988-91.

Whilst Whinchats are widely distributed on Skye, observations over the last few years would tend to suggest that distribution may be sparser than in the past.

STONECHAT   *Saxicola torquatus*   Clacharan (fear na fèill Pàdraig)

Common breeding resident.   **Amber list species.**

Macpherson, somewhat surprisingly, described the Stonechat as a 'summer visitant; thinly distributed over our moorlands'. Both Collier, and later Temperley, found it common on Raasay. Baxter & Rintoul regarded the resident birds which bred commonly on Skye and Raasay as a Hebridean form but this has long since been discredited.

It was confirmed or probably breeding in every square during the 1968-72 and 1988-91 *Atlas* surveys. During the 1981-83 *Winter Atlas* it was recorded in only 13 squares, which may be an indicator of poor coverage.

Stonechats can be strongly territorial throughout the winter and are well distributed. However, it is suspected on Skye, where the breeding population is extremely high, that most juveniles and a significant number of adults are migratory. A count of 10 at the Point of Sleat on 9.9.2004 may be an indicator of this. The *Migration Atlas* suggests that many of the birds which do move, are in Iberia in winter. However, it is also evident that more birds are over-wintering.

NORTHERN WHEATEAR   *Oenanthe oenanthe*   Brù-gheal (clacharan)

Common summer visitor which breeds extensively. Also occurs on passage.

It was 'a summer visitant, arriving at the end of March to nestle in all our glens' according to Macpherson who described it as 'wonderfully numerous' on Waternish. It was found commonly on Raasay between 1200 feet and sea level according to both Collier and Temperley. Baxter & Rintoul regarded it as common on Skye and Raasay.

There was confirmed breeding in virtually every square during the 1968-72 and 1988-91 *Atlas* surveys and this remains a common breeding bird in Skye, unlike other parts of the UK where there has been a marked contraction in breeding range largely due to habitat loss. Most of our population winters in Africa, and most are gone by early September. Birds of the race *leucorhoa* which breed in Greenland and arctic Canada may also occur in Skye during certain weather patterns – slightly larger in size they normally occur later in the autumn. Gerrard caught several examples of this race when he was ringing on Pabay in the 1970s, and an immature of this race was at Waterstein on 24.9.1987 as was a single at Kilmaluag on 1.10.2003. Several examples of this race have been photographed.

This is one of our earliest migrants, with an increasing tendency to arrive as early as mid March. It is also a very noticeable bird on migration, especially at coastal locations, and 25 at Neist Point on 4.8.2001 were obviously south bound migrants.

RING OUZEL   *Turdus torquatus*   Dubh-chreige (lon monaidh)

A summer visitor which breeds, though sparsely.   Red list species.

MacGillivray was first to identify that the species bred on Skye. It was 'A summer visitant, but not numerous, and only nesting sporadically in Skye' according to Macpherson. Collier found it common on Raasay normally arriving in the middle of April. By 1936/37 the Raasay population appeared to have declined significantly, and it was only recorded once by Temperley in 1937. Baxter & Rintoul found it at several sites in 1930 and a nest had been found by Mrs Seton Gordon at Ben Eadarra around 1937.

It was a confirmed or probable breeder in 10 squares during the 1968-72 *Atlas*. In 1982 Church and Lodge thought it was probably breeding at 3 sites in Raasay. There is evidence of a decline in the 1988-91 *Breeding Atlas*, similar to the situation experienced elsewhere in the Highlands. A male near Kensaleyre on 22.12.1986 was either extremely early or extremely late!

A single bird at Loch Ainort on 20.9.2003 was presumably a migrant. Although a number of pairs continue to breed on Skye, especially in the north of the Island, little is known on its current status and distribution. This is unfortunate given its Red list status. However, a record of 4 singing birds on the Trotternish Ridge on 21.5.08 is encouraging.

COMMON BLACKBIRD   *Turdus merula*   Lon dubh (merg)

Common breeding resident and winter visitor.

Macpherson expressed the view that the species had much increased towards the end of the 19th century. In regard to status at that time, Harvie-Brown had suggested it was more numerous as a winter visitor 'haunting the braes above the sea, and other sheltered situations; departing in March'. Writing in 1931 Seton Gordon suggested that in the north of Skye 'the Blackbird was a rarer bird than the Raven'! Later in 1938 he also spoke of a large immigration to northern Skye in November, assuming the birds were of Scandinavian origin. It was found by Baxter & Rintoul in Skye and on Raasay but 'was not as common as the Thrush'.

The species breeds uniformly on Skye on the basis of the 1968-72 *Atlas* results. There was no apparent change in status in 1988-91. During winter, it also appeared to be uniformly distributed according to the 1981-83 *Winter Atlas*. Whilst some of these wintering birds are probably resident, much of the breeding population probably migrates, south and west, possibly into Ireland.

The Blackbird is a common breeding bird on Skye, and certainly appears to be much commoner than it was a century ago. There is still strong evidence of an influx in winter, probably of Scandinavian birds. This often coincides with migrating flocks of Fieldfares and Redwings.

FIELDFARE   *Turdus pilaris*   Liathruisg (uiseag-sneachda)

Common winter visitor and passage migrant.   **Amber list species.**

Macpherson suggested 'large droves frequently occurred on the vernal migration'. On Raasay Collier only found it in small flocks in winter, and these only lingered for a few days.

During the 1988-91 *Breeding Atlas* it was recorded in 6 squares but there was no evidence of breeding and it was suspected that these sightings were of returning winter visitors. However, as the species has now bred in adjacent mainland areas on the west coast it may have been overlooked. It was recorded from 13 squares during the 1981-83 *Winter Atlas* but there was no evidence of large flocks.

Numbers certainly appear to vary from year to year. Most of the birds visiting Skye are passing through but will linger depending on the availability of food, particularly rowan berries. There is an exceptional passage in certain years, October 2003 being an example when many thousands of birds passed through Skye during the middle of the month. It was estimated that there were 10,000 birds in the south of Skye on the 19.10. The best count in 2004 was 1000+ in Harrapool, Broadford, also on 19.10. There was another large influx in 2008 with 2500+ at Camustianavaig in late October.

SONG THRUSH   *Turdus philomelos (hebridensis)*   Smeòrach

Common breeding resident and winter visitor.   **Red list species.**

It was described by Macpherson as a 'prolific resident, nesting in the shrubless Ascrib Islands and in other wild situations'. In the autumn of 1899 Collier had observed a significant influx of Thrushes on Raasay. In November 1937 Seton Gordon observed a similar phenomenon and suggested that considerable numbers of continental thrushes arrived on the western seaboard of Skye.

It was breeding in virtually every square according to the 1968-72 and 1988-91 *Atlas* surveys. There was also a good wintering population with records

from most squares during the 1981-83 *Winter Atlas*.

It is a species which has perhaps benefited from the cover afforded by new coniferous plantations where it breeds extensively. On the basis of observations during the last few years, it certainly appears that the local breeding population, which is significant, is probably migratory, many areas being devoid of Song Thrushes between August and mid October. In late autumn there is a fresh influx of birds often along with Scandinavian thrushes and it is suspected that many of these birds overwinter. Although birds will exploit gardens and croftland to feed, in winter many can also be found on bleak open moorland with no cover whatsoever. In the Garden Wildlife Survey of 2003 it was recorded in 90% of gardens surveyed.

Baxter & Rintoul were first to suggest that the thrushes of Skye and Raasay were of a Hebridean sub-species. The Hebridean form was apparently darker than that found on the mainland and this was accepted by the BOU in 1971, who stated it was confined to the Outer Hebrides and the Isle of Skye. The *Migration Atlas* (2002) also describes the subspecies from the Western Isles and Isle of Skye as *hebridensis*. There is a discussion on Scotland's endemic species in *Scottish Birds* (2003) 24:18-35, which refers specifically to the Song Thrush. This suggests that birds from the Outer Hebrides and Skye are largely sedentary. On the basis of remarks in the previous paragraph, this assertion is questionable, as most breeders disappear by August and start to return in January, being replaced overwinter by what are assumed to be continental thrushes. Unfortunately, because of limited ringing there is little evidence to support these observations. However, there is also little evidence to support the presence of *hebridensis* on Skye.

REDWING   *Turdus ilacus*   Deargan sneachda (sgiath-dheargan)

Common winter visitor and passage migrant.   **Amber list species.**

Macpherson regarded it as a winter visitor but not in large numbers. Although Baxter & Rintoul were able to differentiate an Icelandic form of the species, there is no mention of this in the context of Skye. Collier stated that in some winters large numbers passed through Raasay on their southerly migration.

During the 1968-72 *Breeding Atlas* birds were recorded in 2 squares but breeding was not confirmed. Similarly, during the 1988-91 survey birds were recorded in a number of squares but breeding was not confirmed. Again breeding has been recorded in all the adjacent mainland areas so it may have been overlooked. A bird recorded at Ord on 16.6.1987 was thought to be nesting and there was a late bird on Raasay on 24.5.1998.

The species was recorded in 17 squares during the 1981-83 *Winter Atlas* with some reasonable sized flocks. It is a species which appears to be recorded in some numbers each winter, though many flocks pass through.

According to the *Migration Atlas* the nominate race *iliacus* breeds from Scotland eastwards into Scandinavia. The race *coburni* nests in Iceland and the Faeroes and there is some evidence that birds from eastern Iceland winter in Scotland. It is reasonable to assume that the majority of Redwings seen on Skye are likely to be Icelandic in origin, and on 1.4.2002 a small flock of birds feeding in heathery gullies near Waternish Point flew off north-westwards across the Minch. It may be reasonable to assume that when large mixed flocks of Redwings and Fieldfares occur, as in the autumn of 2003, the Redwings are probably *iliacus,* and Scandinavian in origin.

MISTLE THRUSH   *Turdus viscivorus*   Smeòrach mhor (smeòrach ghlas)

Breeding resident.   **Amber list species.**

Macpherson found it to be resident but scarce in the northern part of the island. Baxter & Rintoul found it nesting sparingly, although it was apparently common in the woods of Raasay. Temperley also found a few pairs nesting around Raasay House.

It was confirmed as breeding in only 6 squares during the 1968-72 *Atlas*, but by the time of the 1988-91 survey some expansion had occurred, with breeding confirmed in a further 4 squares. It was recorded from 10 squares during the 1981-83 *Winter Atlas*, but only in small groups.

This species appears to be much more widespread than previously recorded. It has been recorded breeding widely in forest plantations throughout the island and this may be a factor in this expansion. It gathers in flocks at the end of the breeding season and the best autumn count was 25 at Torrin on 9.9.2001.

COMMON GRASSHOPPER WARBLER   *Locustella naevia*

Summer visitor which breeds – occurs annually in increasing numbers. Red list species.

It was a summer visitant which was scarce according to Macpherson. Baxter & Rintoul did not add to this.

During the 1968-72 *Atlas* there appears to have been confirmed breeding at 1 site and probable breeding at 5 others. It was only recorded in 2 squares in 1988-91 in line with what appeared to be a general decline in numbers throughout Scotland.

There have only been limited reports during the the years up to 2000. Since then singing birds have been recorded annually from a number of widespread localities. In 2003 there were reports from at least 6 separate localities including 2 in forest plantations. Numbers of reports increased further in 2004 suggesting either an expansion of range, or more widespread distribution than previously known. In extensive young plantations near Edinbane there were at least 8 territories in 2004. This wide distribution has been evident since, though annual numbers fluctuate.

SEDGE WARBLER   *Acrocephalus schoenobaenus*   Glaisean (loiliseag)

Summer visitor which breeds in small numbers.

It was regarded as a summer visitant but rare by Macpherson. Likewise, Collier had only a single record for Raasay. Baxter & Rintoul found it breeding in several places. Henson identified the species on 7.3.1956, on Pabay – he had the bird under observation for 30 minutes. Whilst this record was published, it is an exceptionally early date at such a location.

During the 1968-72 *Atlas* there was confirmed or probable breeding from 11 squares. Though it was found breeding in several additional squares in 1988-91, it was absent from a number previously occupied.

It continues to breed in suitable habitats on Skye, albeit in small numbers.

REED WARBLER   *Acrocephalus scirpaceus*

Rare vagrant.

One was trapped and ringed at Borneskitaig, in August 2004. This is the only record for Skye (David Richardson).

BLACKCAP   *Sylvia atricapilla*   Ceann-dubh

Rare summer visitor which probably breeds. Rare winter visitor.

The first record for Skye appears to be a male seen at Portree on 18.11.1952 (*SN* Vol.65 p.58).

There was no record during the 1968-72 *Breeding Atlas* although it was recorded in 4 squares during the 1988-91 survey. There were 2 records during the 1981-83 *Winter Atlas*.

Breeding records for Skye are pretty sparse and there are only a few reports of territorial singing birds.

According to the *Migration Atlas* there is evidence from recoveries that the wintering population is different from the breeding population. Wintering birds are therefore likely to be continental in origin. Whilst this is a scarce bird on Skye, there are more records in winter than in summer. For example there were 10 separate records during the 1983/84 winter (A. Currie pers. comm.). The Dix family have recorded birds regularly in their garden at Rhenetra, Kensaleyre, including 2 pairs on 29.10.1991. Between September – December 1993 there were a number of records from throughout Skye suggesting numbers may vary from year to year. Many of the records on Skye are also October/November and may also be birds which occur as a result of reverse migration, or which 'overshoot' in certain conditions. In the Garden Wildlife Survey of 2003 it was recorded in 14% of gardens surveyed, a remarkable result, although unfortunately there is no indication of when sightings occur. It is interesting to speculate that the birds which visit bird tables in Skye may well be breeding in Eastern Europe.

GARDEN WARBLER *Sylvia borin* Ceileriche gàraidh

Rare summer visitor, probably breeds.

The first record would appear to be a bird caught by T. Gerrard on Pabay in the 1970s, presumably a passage bird. There was no record during the 1968-72 or 1988-91 *Atlas* surveys. However, a bird was reported from a garden at Kensaleyre between 2.-4.5.1988, and again at the same location on 11.9.1999. The most recent report was a singing bird at Waternish on 6.5.2008.

BARRED WARBLER *Sylvia nisoria*

Rare passage migrant.

Described by Harvie-Brown in *The Fauna* as an accidental visitant: 'one was detected by the vigilance of Mr Dumville Lees, who writes to me that he shot an immature bird about a mile from Broadford, August 16th, 1884.' Lees wrote in *The Field* of 1.11.1884: 'We were out after rabbits when I saw a bird quite unknown to me; it was flying from a small bush up a gully' and the specimen was later identified by Mr H. E. Dresser. (Though it met a rather untimely end, it was probably the only way of identifying this scarce vagrant from Eastern Europe, which at the time was the first record for Scotland and only the second for Britain.)

It is not surprising that it was 1971 when the species was next recorded, but quite astonishing that 3 separate birds were trapped on Pabay on 21., 24. and 28.8.

This is a species which regularly overshoots on migration and is recorded in summer and autumn, especially on the eastern seaboard of Scotland. Whilst records are much scarcer from the west coast, there is every possibility that in favourable conditions birds occur but are simply overlooked. The most recent report is of a bird at Dunvegan on 6.10.2001.

LESSER WHITETHROAT   *Sylvia curruca*

Rare passage migrant.

The first report was from Sleat in August 1937. It was then recorded during the 1968-72 *Atlas* in a square in the north of Skye. Unfortunately the authenticity of these records cannot be verified but it is assumed they are accurate.

The *SBR* also reports a bird at Kylerhea on 21.7.1971. More recently there is a record from Portree on 15.9.2007. In 2008 a bird visited feeders in Halistra, Waternish for several weeks from 9.11.2008 (J. Hodgkin & A. Mearns).

COMMON WHITETHROAT   *Sylvia communis*   Gealan coille

Breeds. Summer visitor.

Regarded by Macpherson as a summer visitant, nesting on the banks of wooded burns but rather scarce in north Skye. Collier did not think it bred on Raasay but it did occur on passage. Temperley subsequently found a few pairs breeding on Raasay. In 1930 Baxter & Rintoul found it 'not uncommon' on Skye.

It was confirmed as breeding or probably breeding in 17 squares during the 1968-72 *Atlas*. There was evidence of a decline by 1988-91, in common with other parts of the Highlands.

The Whitethroat remains reasonably well distributed as a breeding bird on Skye.

SUBALPINE WARBLER   *Sylvia cantillans*   Conan coille

Rare vagrant.

On 22.10.2005 one was seen with a mixed feeding flock of Tits and Goldcrests near Dunvegan. This constitutes the first record for Skye. (Geoff Lawson) (HBR).

WOOD WARBLER   *Phylloscopus sibilatrix*   Conan coille

Rare summer visitor which probably breeds.   **Amber list species.**

There was no record in *The Fauna* although it was being increasingly recorded in the nearby mainland by the end of the 19th century. However, Baxter & Rintoul heard a singing bird in the Armadale woods in 1930 and later found 2 pairs in a small wood near Portree, where, according to Murray, 2-3 pairs bred most years. Several pairs were found by Perry in the birch wood above Loch na Béiste.

Though it was not confirmed to breed during the 1968-72 *Atlas*, there were singing birds present in 9 squares, a position which appeared to have worsened by 1988-91. Thom stated that the species bred at least sporadically on Skye.

There continue to be reports from sites where there is suitable breeding habitat, though records remain sparse.

COMMON CHIFFCHAFF   *Phylloscopus collybita*   Caifean

Rare summer visitor which probably breeds.

Macpherson encountered a single bird of the species which 'he met on migration at Bracadale' in April 1889, seemingly the only record until Temperley found several singing regularly in the woods and plantations around Raasay House in 1936/37.

It was confirmed as breeding or probably breeding in 3 squares during the 1968-72 *Atlas* and was equally scarce in 1988-91. Thom observed sporadic breeding on Skye and Raasay. There was a single winter record during the 1981-83 *Winter Atlas*, which is extremely interesting, but no details are available.

There continues to be a scattering of singing birds from a variety of localities each year. Passage birds or vagrants may also occur and there is a record from Pabay in the 1970s, from Borve on 10.11.1978, and more recently a late bird at Harrapool on 6.11.2003. There are increasing winter records from Scotland and a report of a bird foraging in a garden at Lower Milovaig, Glendale, on 27.12.2004 was extremely unusual. Several late birds were seen in 2005 including a bird showing characterisitics of the race abietinus.

WILLOW WARBLER   *Phylloscopus trochilus*   Crionag ghiuthais

Very common summer visitor which breeds extensively.
Amber list species.

Macpherson suggested it was a summer visitor, decidedly local, and much scarcer than in Eigg and Mull. Temperley found it one of the most abundant species on Raasay, very similar to Baxter & Rintoul who also found it 'abundant' on Skye.

During the 1968-72 and 1988-91 *Atlas* surveys it was recorded as breeding in most squares.

This remains an extremely common breeding bird on Skye. The main arrivals are from mid April, though there is an early date of 7.4.2002. The latest date recorded was 11.10.2002 at Harrapool.

GOLDCREST *Regulus regulus*   Crionag bhuidhe (dreathan a' chinn bhuidhe)

Common breeding resident.   **Amber list species.**

According to Gray it was frequent in Skye in the late 19th century especially where larches had been planted. Likewise, Macpherson found it resident in the larger woodlands, but not very numerous. Collier found it plentiful in the fir woods at the south of Raasay, greatly increased numbers being observed in late autumn. It was found by Baxter & Rintoul in Skye and Raasay.

During the 1968-72 *Atlas* it was confirmed breeding in 11 squares and by 1988-91 there appeared to have been some expansion. Thom noted this expansion, suggesting it was the result of continued afforestation. There were only records from 8 squares during the 1981-83 *Winter Atlas*.

There would appear to have been little change in status in recent years. The distribution of the Goldcrest is closely linked to that of coniferous planting and it is reasonable to point to expansion of range in line with the spread of coniferous plantations.

SPOTTED FLYCATCHER   *Muscicapa striata*   Breacan sgiobalt (glac nan cuileag)

Summer visitor which breeds.   **Red list species.**

Macpherson suggested that it was a summer visitant nesting at several localities and decidedly increasing. Collier was aware of 5 pairs breeding on Raasay in 1901 though Temperley found none in 1936/37. Baxter & Rintoul stated it bred commonly on Skye.

It was confirmed breeding in 16 squares during the 1968-72 *Atlas*. Whilst there was an apparent decline in breeding records in Skye during the 1988-91 survey, this may have reflected observer coverage.

Little is known on the present status of this species. However, there is no indication that its range has significantly altered.

RED-BREASTED FLYCATCHER   *Ficedula parva*

Scarce vagrant.

The first record for Skye was of a female seen by the Dix family at Staffin on 31.10.1982. There is a further report from Dunvegan Castle on 6.10.2001. This is a vagrant which occurs regularly in Scotland, most occurrences resulting from birds undertaking reverse migration.

PIED FLYCATCHER   *Ficedula hypoleuca*   Breacan glas

Very rare summer visitor. No recent breeding record.

There is no historical record. During the 1968-72 *Breeding Atlas* it was found in 3 squares and these appear to be the first records for the island. Church and Lodge found it on Raasay in 1982 when Andrew Currie also had records in Skye (WHFP). It was also found at 2 squares in the 1988-91 *Breeding Atlas*.

The only recent records appear to be a single at Uig Hotel, Skye, on 6.6.1995, and a male in suitable breeding habitat in Sleat on 12.6.1999.

LONG-TAILED TIT   *Aegithalos caudatus*   Cìochan (mionntan)

Common breeding resident.

Gray suggests it was rather common in parts of Skye though Macpherson noted only that it was resident and observed occasionally. Collier found it common and resident on Raasay. Baxter & Rintoul regarded it as breeding sparingly on Skye as well as Raasay.

During the 1968-72 *Breeding Atlas* it was confirmed in 9 squares, mainly in the south of the island and that continued to be the pattern in 1988-91. However, during the 1981-83 *Winter Atlas* it was recorded in 8 squares, 3 of which were in the north of the island including Raasay. Thom suggested it was not too numerous but widespread.

There is no indication of change in status, and some evidence that the species still favours the south of the island although there was a large flock of 20 at Portree on 14.11.2002. It is a bird which is often more conspicuous during autumn and winter when noisy flocks are on the move. These can be encountered in quite remote localities suggesting flocks range widely in winter.

WILLOW TIT   *Parus montanus*

Historical record only.

Collier records the Marsh-Titmouse on Raasay 'only occasionally observed during bad weather in the winter, generally in the company with other Tits'. Baxter & Rintoul point to possible confusion between Marsh and Willow Tit, and although they do not comment on Collier's Raasay records, it is most likely that his observations related to the Willow Tit which at that time bred in the Highlands. Baxter & Rintoul refer to breeding records from Loch Maree in 1921, Achnacarry in 1938, and Inverpolly in 1942. It is therefore quite conceivable that in bad weather birds might wander west on to Raasay or that a small remnant population bred, undetected by Collier. Thom (1986) quotes Roy Dennis as suggesting that the Highland populations may have suffered as a result of the bad winters in the late 1940s and early 1950s, because the species is now confined to the southern part of Scotland.

COAL TIT   *Parus ater*   Smutag (cailleachag cheann dubh)

Common breeding resident.

Gray records it in the woods of Skye. It is described in *The Fauna* as resident and fairly common in the Dunvegan woods. According to both Collier and Temperley, it was the commonest of titmice on Raasay. It was widely seen by Baxter & Rintoul in Skye and Raasay.

The species was confirmed breeding in 14 squares during the 1968-72 *Atlas* and this was slightly increased in 1988-91. Surprisingly, it was only recorded in 10 squares during the 1981-83 *Winter Atlas*. A. Currie (in Thom 1986) suggested it was widespread but still not numerous on Skye.

With wide afforestation, there is no shortage of suitable habitat for this species. A succession of mild winters may also have assisted survival rates. The Coal Tit would certainly appear to be widely distributed and a regular visitor to most bird tables.

BLUE TIT   *Parus caeruleus*   Cailleachag cheann-ghorm (snoileun)

Common breeding resident.

Described in *The Fauna* as resident, it would not appear to have been particularly common towards the end of the 19th century. However, Collier found it was quite common on Raasay. Baxter & Rintoul also found it well distributed.

During the 1968-72 and 1988-91 *Atlas* surveys it appears to have been breeding in 80% of squares. It was recorded in 17 squares during the 1981-83 *Winter Atlas*.

Though little is known on current breeding success or expansion of range, the Blue Tit is commonly distributed on Skye. In the Garden Wildlife Survey of 2003 it was found in 92% of gardens surveyed.

GREAT TIT   *Parus major*   Currac bhaintighearna

Common breeding resident.

It was described only as a 'casual visitant' by Macpherson and appears to have been first seen on the island during the winter of 1884-85. It was uncommon on Raasay according to Collier but a few pairs bred every year. Interestingly, by 1936/37 the Raasay population was found by Temperley to be well established. Baxter & Rintoul found a good many there in 1926 and subsequently found them breeding in Kyleakin and Portree. According to Mrs Seton Gordon they were widely distributed by the 1950s.

It was recorded as a confirmed breeder in 23 *Atlas* squares in 1968-72. The status was little changed in 1988-91. There were winter records from 18 squares during the 1981-83 *Winter Atlas*.

This species has therefore successfully colonised Skye during the last 100 years. It adapts easily to a whole range of habitats and has probably been helped by afforestation. In the Garden Wildlife Survey of 2003 it was found in 86% of the gardens surveyed.

149

WOOD NUTHATCH   *Sitta europaea*

Historical record only.

The Fauna provides an account of two birds which appeared at Waternish in the spring of 1885 'haunting the trees around the house' and which were apparently quite tame. The birds were seen by Captain MacDonald who appears to have provided a satisfactory description which was accepted by Harvie-Brown, who regarded it as a casual visitant. This record also seems to have been accepted by Baxter & Rintoul.

EURASIAN TREECREEPER   *Certhia familiaris*   Snàigear (meanglan)

Breeding resident.

Gray could find no trace of the species in the Inner Hebrides. However, Macpherson certainly regarded it as resident and probably of general distribution. Collier found it numerous on Raasay. Baxter & Rintoul found it breeding at Broadford and Dunvegan in 1930 and it was later found in the Kyleakin area and on Raasay.

The species was only confirmed to breed in 5 squares during the 1968-72 *Atlas* but in 1988-91 there was some evidence of expansion to the north of the island. It was recorded in 7 squares, including 3 in the north of the island during the 1981-83 *Winter Atlas*.

There is no current evidence of any change in status.

GOLDEN ORIOLE   *Oriolus oriolus*

Very rare vagrant.

The only record was a female at Pooltiel Pier on 19.5.1986.

RED-BACKED SHRIKE   *Lanius collurio*

Very rare vagrant.

Surprisingly, the only record to date appears to be a first year bird at Duntulm Hotel on 10.9.1988.

GREAT GREY SHRIKE   *Lanius excubitor*

Very rare passage migrant and winter visitor.

In a Scottish context this species is much more common on autumn passage and as a winter visitor. It is therefore surprising that there is no historical information and the first record appears to be from Raasay on 5.5.1984. In

June 1985 singles were recorded from 3 separate locations, possibly the same bird. There is a report from Glen Brittle on 13.3.1986. The only autumn record traced was a bird between Penifiler and Camastianavaig on 25.10.1997.

WOODCHAT SHRIKE   *Lanius senator*

Scarce vagrant.

In 1988 an adult was at Trotternish between 1-3 June, and presumably the same bird was present at Waternish between 18-19 June. This was an amazing enough record in itself, but in 1989, a single bird was recorded at Dunvegan on 1 June, then at Struan on 28 June. Was this the 1988 bird returning yet again, trying to find a mate? Given that the nearest breeders are in France and Spain these were extremely unusual records.

BLACK-BILLED MAGPIE   *Pica pica*   Pioghaid (athaid)

Very rare migrant historically. May have bred more recently.

Macpherson recorded this species, which was seen at Waternish in May 1882 by Captain MacDonald. Baxter & Rintoul mention a further record at Kyleakin on 7.1.1883, the source of which is not known.

During the 1968-72 *Atlas* it appears to have been recorded on 2 squares in Raasay, well outwith its normal range, and *SBR* 1972 refers to a nest at Braes on 29.5.1972. In the summer of 1976 a bird was again on Raasay and perhaps the same bird was in Portree during the autumn of that year.

There were singles at Kilmuir 6.5.1988, Neist Point on 11.6.1990 and nearby Waterstein on 14.10.1991. There was a long gap but single birds have now been recorded in the last few years..

RED-BILLED CHOUGH   *Pyrrhocorax pyrrhocorax*   Cathag dhearg-chasach

Has bred, but no recent records.   **Amber list species.**

The Isle of Skye seems to have been the northern limit of its range on the west coast of Scotland where it bred in 'limited numbers'. Gray had seen a clutch of 3 eggs in a collection which had been removed from Skye in the mid 19th century. At the time of the *The Fauna* there were still a number of pairs breeding on both the east and west coasts, though Captain MacDonald of Waternish's assertion that there were 20 pairs on his estate in 1890 does seem a slight exaggeration! Collier had only two records for Raasay, both in January, 1898, involving a few birds which he assumed were 'wandering'. In 1926 Baxter & Rintoul were informed that birds used to nest near Flodigarry but none had been seen since the 1914-18 war. Apparently a pair had left their sea cliff site and nested in the chimney of an occupied house. It had also nested on Raasay.

It therefore appears that this species disappeared as a breeding bird from Skye around 1918. As Gray has earlier suggested, the Chough was at the northern limit of its range and hung on in Skye longer than elsewhere. The exact cause of its decline has never been properly explained, egg collectors, over zealous 'keepers, Peregrines and Jackdaws all being suggested as possible factors. It was suggested by Murray that a friend had seen a bird below the Storr Rocks in 1953. This could have been a wandering bird, but the Chough does not appear to have been recorded on the island until 4.5.2005 when a single bird was observed on Raasay (Mathew Wilson).

EURASIAN JACKDAW   *Corvus monedula*   Cathag (cnàimh-fhitheach)

Common breeding resident.

It was described by Macpherson as resident, but scarce. A few pairs bred on Raasay where Collier found numbers increased in winter. In 1930 Baxter & Rintoul found it 'local and scarce in most places but breeding plentifully in the north head of Portree' where it was again found to be numerous in 1939. A small colony was breeding on Raasay in 1904 but not seen by Temperley in 1936 or 1937.

During the 1968-72 *Atlas* there was confirmed breeding in 11 squares and there was little change in 1988-91. The Jackdaw was recorded in 14 squares during the 1981-83 *Winter Atlas* with a bias towards the north of the island. From the *Migration Atlas* it is apparent that some of these wintering birds may be Scandinavian breeders. On 17.10.2003 a party of 55 Jackdaws were seen circling 1000 feet above Point of Sleat, which appeared to be birds on the move.

ROOK   *Corvus frugilegus*   Ròcas (creumhach)

Common breeding resident.

Gray recorded a large rookery at Dunvegan which he suggested was the most westerly in the UK. It was only recently established and the trees were small. Later, Macpherson suggested it was resident and increasing, highlighting about 8 rookeries throughout the island. Collier suggested a large rookery on Raasay was 'done away with' between 1890 and 1902 because of the harm they did by 'sucking the eggs of Grouse'! Baxter & Rintoul reported several rookeries in 1930, the largest being in Portree, and 535 nests were recorded on the island in 1945. Though formerly breeding at Raasay House, it was then absent as a breeding bird in 1936 and Temperley suggested that the large rookery was destroyed between 1890 and 1902 'in the interests of game' – this is an indicator of the length of time a species takes to establish itself after local eradication.

There was confirmed breeding in 7 squares during the 1968-72 *Atlas* and perhaps a slight decrease in 1988-91. In the 1975 census a total of 420 nests were recorded, with 89 nests at Husabost, the largest rookery. The species is more dispersed in winter with records from 17 squares during the 1981-83 *Winter Atlas*.

There is no current knowledge on any change in status or range. A strain of 'Brown' Rooks has been evident in the Portree area for the last 25 years - probably best described as Leucistic.

CARRION CROW   *Corvus corone*   Feannag

Regular vagrant and may have bred.

Macpherson provided evidence of 'definite' examples of this species in 1885 and 1889. Likewise, Collier had a record for 1897 on Raasay.

During the 1968-72 *Atlas* there was a single confirmed breeding record of Carrion Crow. Similarly, there were records of Carrion breeding in 2 squares in 1988-91. Carrion was recorded in 3 squares during the 1981-83 *Winter Atlas*.

It is only recently that the Carrion Crow has been 'split' from the Hooded and is now regarded as a separate species. Though a common breeding bird on the east coast, the *Atlas* breeding records above are extremely interesting but cannot be verified. However, small groups of 'pure' Carrion Crows have been recorded in Strathaird in the late summer of 2002 and 2003 and singles regularly at several locations.

HOODED CROW   *Corvus cornix*   Feannag Ghlas (feannag chorrach)

Very common breeding resident.

It was resident and, according to Macpherson, despite being an 'expert oophilist and oologist, the Hoodie feeds largely on fish offal and flotsam and jetsam.' However, it had become scarce in some districts, because, as Macpherson eloquently suggests 'they are met with scant courtesy: their note is an instruction to murder – "where are they and how can we get a shot at them?" is the usual question'. Collier found them very common on Raasay. Later, Temperley wrote vociferously:

> These birds are the curse of the island, for they have multiplied so rapidly as to have overrun the whole of it, and the gamekeeper is quite unable to keep them in check. The keeper holds the hooded-crows mainly responsible for the practical extermination of the pheasants

and blackgame, and for the great reduction in the number of red grouse, all of which were once so plentiful, and they are without doubt also responsible for the very small number of other ground nesting birds now breeding on the island.

(Temperley did not record Golden Eagles during his visits to Raasay in 1936/37 – one can only assume that the keeper managed to keep them 'in check'!)

During the 1968-72 and the 1988-91 *Breeding Atlas* Hooded Crows were breeding in every square. They were similarly well distributed during the 1981-83 *Winter Atlas*. The Hooded Crow breeds extensively on Skye and remains the subject of much heated debate in terms of the level of damage done to young birds and eggs, particularly of waders and Red Grouse. In regard to the latter, on the Eilean Iarmain Estate crow traps are used to manage the population and some 1600 birds have been destroyed over a 6 year period.

COMMON RAVEN   *Corvus corax*   Fitheach (biadhtach)

Common breeding resident.

In spite of persecution Gray reported that the species continued to breed up to 1870. *The Fauna* describes widescale persecution, but despite this Macpherson suggests it can maintain 'a footing in our midst by its natural craftiness, to-gether with the precipitous character of the cliffs which it favours for nesting'. Collier found a few pairs nesting on Raasay and its status there was unchanged when Temperley visited in 1936/37.

It was confirmed breeding in most squares during the 1968-72 and 1988-91 *Atlas* surveys. Similarly in winter the species is well distributed being found in good numbers in most squares during 1981-83.

The Raven remains an extremely common breeding bird on Skye. For example, on the Strathaird peninsula, which extends to 2,500 hectares, there is a minimum of 6 breeding pairs, which nest on both coastal and inland cliffs. Tree nesting has also been found on Skye. It is not unusual to see large groups of birds together. A communal roost in larch trees near Portree held 100+ birds on 25.1.2002 and 60+ birds on 18.12.2004. Large numbers of birds formerly frequented the refuse disposal site near Portree where up to 150 have been counted. However, this site has now closed.

COMMON STARLING   *Sturnus vulgaris*   Druid

Common breeding resident and winter visitor.   **Red list species.**

According to *The Fauna* it was resident, nesting in the crevices of cliffs and among old buildings. Macpherson stated the species had vastly increased in numbers since 1892. It is significant that Gray did not mention them at all, suggesting they colonised post 1870. Collier also found them on Raasay saying they increased in the autumn. Baxter & Rintoul found them well distributed on the island in 1930.

During the 1968-72 *Atlas* it was confirmed breeding in most squares, though there seems to have been a slight decline in 1988-91. During the 1981-83 *Winter Atlas* it was recorded from most squares in the north of the island but few in the south. It is suspected this was a question of coverage as birds seem to be widely distributed in winter.

Whilst roost sites never reach the proportions of many urban areas, small roosts occur in caves throughout the coastline. Wintering flocks tend to be small, so 500 at Kilmaluag on 19.12.2003 was unusual.

ROSY STARLING   *Sturnus roseus*

Rare vagrant but has occurred in recent irruptions.

Macpherson stated that a bird had been shot 'some years ago', possibly in the 1870s by Captain Cameron, at Glen Brittle.

Since then there have only been a few reports, all of singles, e.g. from Harlosh on 10.8.1984. A bird at Portree from 7-9.8.1996 was photographed and accepted by BBRC. There was a report from Glendale on 30.9.2000 and a further reliable report from Orbost in July 2002, at which time there was a big irruption. There was a juvenile at Ferindonald on 8.10.2005. (HBR)

HOUSE SPARROW   *Passer domesticus*   Glaisean (gealbhonn)

Common breeding resident.   **Red list species.**

It was regarded as a common resident which seemed to have rapidly increased in numbers and extended its range according to Macpherson. Collier and Temperley found it numerous on Raasay. According to Baxter & Rintoul it increased during the first half of the 20th century and is now common, 'and is a resident in varying numbers in Raasay'.

The species was well distributed at the time of the 1968-72 *Atlas* with confirmed breeding in most squares. However, it was apparently absent from several squares in 1988-91 where it had previously been confirmed as breeding. During the 1981-83 *Winter Atlas* it was found in 16 squares, but was surprisingly absent from others where it obviously bred during the summer months.

Though House Sparrows continue to be well distributed on Skye, this is perhaps very much dependent on the continuing availability of suitable buildings for nesting. However, it can be local in its distribution. For example, although it breeds in Torrin, it is sparse in Elgol a few miles away. Perhaps it does not favour the exposed nature of some localities.

EURASIAN TREE SPARROW   *Passer montanus*   Gealbhonn nan craobh

Has bred, but no recent records so status unknown.   Red list species.

It is 'doubtless resident' according to Macpherson, a positive record from Uig in 1886 being the only supporting evidence. A few pairs were apparently found on Raasay by Collier between 1896-1902 but none were seen subsequently.

A group of 8 was recorded at Torrin in 1937. The species appears to be recorded in 2 squares during the 1968-72 *Atlas* with confirmed breeding in one. There was apparently confirmed breeding in only one square in 1988-91.

Unfortunately, no opportunity has been available to follow up these *Atlas* records. Thom regarded it as 'local and sporadic' on Skye, but also highlighted that it was absent from most of the West Highlands. This species has experienced a significant crash in numbers elsewhere. That a small remnant population in Skye could survive, given the recent changes in farming and crofting practices, is highly unlikely. However, there have been reports from Dunvegan and a single bird appeared at a garden feeder at Lower Milovaig on 2.5.2008 (A. Stables).

CHAFFINCH   *Fringilla coelebs*   Breacan-beithe (breacan baintighearna)

Common breeding resident. Winter visitor.

A numerous resident, though most abundant in winter, when large flocks of both sexes appear. Macpherson also noted that where trees were scarce their nests would be almost on the ground or on a low cliff. Collier found it to be a common resident on Raasay. It was later said to be common on Skye and Raasay by Baxter & Rintoul.

It was uniformly distributed at the time of the 1968-72 and 1988-91 *Breeding Atlas* surveys. It was recorded from most low ground squares during the 1981-83 *Winter Atlas*.

This is a common breeding bird which has taken advantage of the extensive afforestation experienced on the island to extend its range. The presence of Brambling in some of the flocks which occur in winter also suggests that continental birds may visit Skye. Winter flocks do not reach the scale found on the mainland, and 200+ at Kensaleyre on 3.11.1982 was unusual. Coincidentally there was a similar count at the same location on 15.11.2003.

BRAMBLING   *Fringilla montifringilla*   Bricein caorainn (lùth-eun)

An irregular winter visitor in small numbers.

There was no record from Skye in either *The Fauna* or *The Birds of Scotland*. Collier however, had recorded 7-8 on Raasay with Chaffinches in February 1900, during hard frost and snow.

The species was recorded in 4 squares during the 1981-83 *Winter Atlas*.

Recently, birds have been recorded in most winters, anytime from late October onwards. However, most have been in penny numbers, usually accompanying flocks of Chaffinches.

EUROPEAN GREENFINCH   *Carduelis chloris*   Glaisean daraich (corcan glas)

Common breeding resident.

Described by Macpherson as a 'winter visitant and the flocks which gather round farm buildings linger into April' – there was seemingly no evidence of breeding at that time. Collier however, had an occasional pair breeding in the shrubberies on Raasay. The first breeding record for the main island would appear to be by Baxter & Rintoul, who in 1930 found a pair feeding young at Portree. Breeding birds were also found at Broadford and Kyleakin suggesting it had become much more widespread.

By the time of the 1968-72 *Atlas* the Greenfinch was well established as a breeding bird being confirmed in 20 squares. However, by 1988-91 there appeared to have been a local contraction in numbers, though this may reflect poor coverage. It was recorded in only 9 squares during the 1981-83 *Winter Atlas*.

This is another species which flocks in winter and P. Ellis recorded a flock of 60 near Loch Snizort Beag on 15.10.1978. Thom refers to a winter flock of 200 on Skye in December, 1981. Even by current standards these flocks are large. However, the species remains a well-stablished breeding resident and in the Garden Wildlife Survey of 2003 it was found in 79% of gardens surveyed.

EUROPEAN GOLDFINCH   *Carduelis carduelis*   Deargan fraoich

Breeding resident and some evidence of expansion.

Macpherson regarded the species as an irregular visitor in autumn to the south of Skye, although there had been a breeding record. Collier had a pair breeding on Raasay in 1897 and 1898 but they disappeared after that. It seems to have been a rare bird at the turn of the 19th century and even on the publication of *The Birds of Scotland* in 1953 by Baxter & Rintoul, there was little more to add.

During the 1968-72 Atlas it was recorded in one square. Reed *et al.* did not include the Goldfinch as a breeding species for Skye in their paper of 1983. The 1988-91 *Atlas* confirmed breeding at 2 sites. This lack of breeding records is interesting given that it was recorded in 6 squares during the 1981-83 *Winter Atlas*. Reed and later Thom failed to note the earlier 1968-72 record which appears to signal the beginning of what appears to be slow but substantial expansion in range. This is confirmed by records from Bruce Philp who had recorded birds at Portree in 1975 and 1977. More significantly however, he recorded winter flocks at Skeabost of 15 on 15.11.1980 and 30 on 20.3.1982, a good indicator that the species was doing well.

During the last few years it has been noted regularly at various parts of the island, invariably in small numbers, the best 'charms' being 8 at Dunvegan on 12.11.2001 and 11 at Broadford 23.11.2001. It would appear that 2003 was an exceptional breeding year with a flock of 30 at Harrapool on 26.11.and possibly the same flock at Breakish on 29.11. In Strathaird there were flocks of 20 at Glasnakille on 16.10 and at Torrin on 22.10. The best charm of the lot was a superb 40 at Geary on 17.11.2003. There was a similar number along with other finches in Dunvegan on 15.11.2004. In the Garden Wildlife Survey of 2003 it had been recorded in 49% of gardens surveyed, a reflection on how well the species is established. Numbers have increased in the last few years with a flock of 70 at Roag on 19.10.2008 reflecting this.

EURASIAN SISKIN   *Carduelis spinus*   Gealag bhuidhe

Common breeding resident. Passage migrant

Macpherson had no records from Skye in *The Fauna* although Baxter & Rintoul refer to large numbers at Kyleakin, Skye, in November, 1886.

Reed *et al.* suggested that the Siskin colonised Skye in the 1960s and certainly during the 1968-72 *Atlas* there was either confirmed or probable breeding in 6 squares and this was further increased in 1988-91. During the 1981-83 *Winter Atlas*, it was only found in 3 squares, possibly implying that local breeding birds migrate.

The Siskin now breeds widely on Skye, an expansion which may have been helped by afforestation. This is confirmed by the 2003 Garden Wildlife Survey which recorded Siskins in 57% of gardens. That said, there are few records of flocks of any size, 40 at Ord on 31.10.1985 and 30 at Torrin on 7.9.2002, being amongst the few examples.

COMMON LINNET   *Carduelis cannabina*   Gealan lin (didig)

Localised breeding bird and passage migrant.   **Red list species.**

Although Macpherson regarded it as resident, but probably scarce, there only seems to have been a single record from Broadford to support this. Collier, 1896-1902, had found several pairs nesting on a patch of gorse on Raasay, but they were not seen subsequently by Temperley. During their various visits to the island, the only record by Baxter & Rintoul was a single bird at Sconser in 1930.

It was only recorded in 5 squares during the 1968-72 *Atlas* and probably bred in 3. If anything, the situation was poorer in 1988-91 with evidence of birds in only 4 squares. It was recorded in 4 squares in the 1981-83 *Winter Atlas*, including a flock of 30+ birds.

Inexperienced observers and visitors to Skye have a tendency to confuse this species with its much more common relative the Twite. By comparison, the Linnet does not appear to have ever been common or widespread on Skye but there has probably been a further decline. There may still be small pockets of suitable habitat where birds breed and there have been regular reports from Aird Bernisdale. There were reports of a single bird at Harrapool on 13.4 and 2.7.2002, which might suggest possible breeding in the area. In 2003 a single bird was seen on 2 occasions in June near Struan. A party of 7 at Point of Sleat on 20.9.2003 were probably migrants. Numbers may have increased since 2003 and there have been several breeding records. There was a feeding flock of 30 at Ashaig on 6.8.2007.

TWITE   *Carduelis flavirostris*   Riabhag mhonaidh/fhraoich
(gealan-beinne, bigein baintighearna)

Breeds commonly – main population absent in winter. Red list species.

It was described in *The Fauna* as 'Resident, gathering into flocks of from a dozen, to more than a hundred birds in autumn, and flocking late into spring.' Collier found it nesting yearly on Raasay but in sparse numbers. Baxter & Rintoul found Twites nesting in Skye in 1910, 1930 and 1939 and it was also breeding in small colonies in Raasay in 1937.

It was found to be uniformly distributed by the time of the 1968-72 *Atlas*, confirmed or probable breeding in most squares. There was little change in 1988-91. It is only recorded in 5 squares during the 1981-83 *Winter Atlas*, all of which are in the north of the island, including a flock of 70+ birds. In 1983 Reed *et al.* suggested that Twite appeared to have declined in abundance and distribution and suggested that this might be due to agricultural and crofting changes. In 1987/88 there were several records of winter flocks of 30-40 birds in January and February all in the north of the island.

A significant proportion of the breeding population is thought to migrate, and from early November until March, Twite are scarce. The only evidence to suggest where the birds winter is a single recovery of a bird ringed on Pabay in early August, which moved south-west to Northern Ireland where it was trapped in February of the following year. Some observations at Point of Sleat and Strathaird Point would tend to support this south-westwards movement, as visible daytime migration can be observed. To complicate matters however, on 11.10.2003 a party of 9 flew west over the sea at Neist Point, seemingly heading for the Uists.

In late summer and autumn birds gather into feeding flocks, some of which become quite large. Examples include 140+ Pabay on 25.8.1972 and c200 at Kilmaluag on 9.10.1978. Counts in 2003 were high, perhaps reflecting a good breeding season with 170 at Harrapool on 27.9, and exceptional counts of 300 at Harrapool on 5.10 and 350+ at Ardroag on 8.10. In 2004 there were equally large numbers with 220 at Harrapool on 12.10 and 260 at Ardroag on 10.10. There is certainly little indication at this time that Twite numbers are in decline on Skye and the population seems to be healthy. Given the threats to the species elsewhere, the Skye population is extremely important.

LESSER REDPOLL   *Carduelis cabaret*   Deargan seilich

Common breeding resident. Passage migrant.   **Amber list species.**

There were several breeding records in the 1880s from Macpherson, who regarded it as a summer visitor. Collier found it common on Raasay. In 1930 Baxter & Rintoul found it 'unexpectedly plentiful in both natural and planted wood' even on the hazel scrub right on on the west point of Portree. They also spoke of a small colony on Raasay.

During the 1968-72 *Atlas*, there was confirmed breeding in 7 squares, although some evidence of a decline in 1988-91. During the 1981-83 *Winter Atlas* it was only recorded in 2 squares.

The above records are difficult to reconcile given the current widespread distribution, especially in forestry plantations. Little is known of the population in winter but it is reasonable to assume that a significant proportion of breeding birds are migratory.

COMMON CROSSBILL   *Loxia curvirostra*   Cam-ghob (deargan giuthais)

Breeding resident in small numbers.

The first record from Skye appears to be 28.7.1888 when Dumville Lees writing in *The Field* reported a flock of 12, location not given. Collier saw several flocks on Raasay during the 1896 winter and also found it breeding in 1898, 1899 and 1901. Baxter & Rintoul do not contribute further to the historical record.

There were no records during the 1968-72 *Breeding Atlas* survey. In 1983 Reed *et al.* did not include Crossbill as breeding on Skye and neither did Thom shortly afterwards. However, during the 1988-91 *Breeding Atlas* there is evidence of breeding from 1 square, possibly the first confirmed record for Skye. It was also present in another square.

As far as winter records were concerned, Pete Ellis had recorded 2 at Glen Brittle on 7.10.1978 and 3 at Loch a' Ghlinne on 6.12.1978. During the 1981-83 *Winter Atlas* birds were recorded in 2 squares.

In the intervening years birds have continued to be recorded although always in small numbers, and from a wide range of localities invariably associated with forest plantings. There was a flock of 20+ on Raasay on 21.1.1991. A flock of 10 was recorded in Glen Eynort on 3.12.1998. In 2002 there was proved breeding at Kyleakin with fledged young being seen on 10.5. During other work by the author in forest plantations in 2003 it became apparent how well established and widespread the population is. Though difficult to quantify in numbers, a significant Crossbill population appears to have colonised Skye in the last 20 years.

COMMON ROSEFINCH   *Carpodacus erythrinus*

Scarce Vagrant.

There is a report of a single bird in the trees at Tormore, Sleat, on 9.6.1984 (per A. Currie). There is also a report of a bird at Dunvegan on 6-7.10.2003. A male visited a garden in Kyleakin on 25.5.2008 (A & E Horner).

COMMON BULLFINCH   *Pyrrhula pyrrhula*   Deargan coille (corran coille)

Common breeding resident.

Although Macpherson had only a single record from Greshornish, it was a resident, breeding in the Sleat area. A few scattered pairs bred on Raasay according to Collier. In 1930 Baxter & Rintoul also found it in Sleat, at Armadale, and a pair bred near Kyleakin. In 1939 it was found to be common on Raasay. It was also found by Perry near Kyleakin.

There was either confirmed or probable breeding in 13 *Atlas* squares between 1968-72. There was little change in 1988-91. During the 1981-83 *Winter Atlas* it was only recorded in 6 squares, all in the south of the island.

Bullfinches appear to do quite well in Skye. In particular, it is a species which has adapted extremely well to breeding in forest plantations. It also frequents gardens and was recorded in 44% of those sampled in the 2003 Garden Wildlife Survey.

During the late autumn of 2004 there was a significant influx of 'northern' Bullfinches to Scotland. A group of 4 near Broadford on 19.12 showed strong characteristics of these birds which probably originate in Scandinavia.

HAWFINCH   *Coccothraustes coccothraustes*

Scarce vagrant.

During the last few years there have been an increasing number of occurrences on the west of Scotland. A report from the grounds of the Cuillin Hills Hotel at Portree on 6.5.2004 is the first known record for Skye. There was a single at a bird feeder at Kyleakin on 22.4.2005 and another in a garden in Glen Brittle on 1.6.2008.

BLACKPOLL WARBLER   *Dendroica stiata*

Palearctic Vagrant.

This is a north American breeding species and an immature found at Glasnakille on 4.10.2005 was the first record for the Highland recording area and the seventh record for Scotland. (R. McMillan, R. Day)

LAPLAND LONGSPUR (BUNTING)   *Calcarious lapponicus*

Rare passage migrant.

The first records for Skye appear to be a small flock at Braes on 25.9.1977 and a flock found in Trotternish during the 1981-83 *Winter Atlas*, further

162

details of which are not available. There is however a record of a male in breeding plumage at Staffin on 4.4.1981. It has also been recorded recently at Elgol, when at least one, possibly two birds were seen on 17.3.2002. A male was seen at Elgol on 7.4.2008.

SNOW BUNTING   *Plectrophenax nivalis*   Gealag/eun an t-sneachda

A winter visitor in small numbers.   **Amber list species.**

According to Macpherson it was a winter visitor, with several records in the 1880s. Collier confirmed this for Raasay saying that small flocks tended to come and go with snow storms.

In late August, 1932, a cock in full breeding plumage was seen near the top of Sgurr nan Gillean. Seton Gordon and Niall Rankin saw a flock near the summit of Bruach na Frithe on 2.5.1936 'but these were almost certainly migrants'. Although Nethersole-Thompson (1966) stated that there is no confirmed breeding record for Skye, in June 1972 a male was seen on stony scree above 2500 feet on Sgurr Alasdair, so there is just the possibility that birds may have bred in the Cuillin.

Best winter counts include 30 at Braes on 8.11.1978, 23 at Duntulm on 2.12.1978 and 25 at Kensalyre on 3.2.1980. It was recorded in 6 squares during the 1981-83 *Winter Atlas* and the *Migration Atlas* would tend to support the argument that many of these birds are from Iceland. The biggest count was 120 on the Lealt River in late December 2001. There were 14 on Marsco on 3.4.1988 and 30+ on Ben Aslak on 17.1.2004 but most recent records have been of small numbers. A pair spent April 2008 at the author's house in Elgol, feeding in the garden and perching on the roof.

YELLOWHAMMER   *Emberiza citrinella*   Buidheag (buidhean na coille)

Formerly bred commonly, now rare and local.   **Red list species.**

In the second part of the 19th century Gray found the species on all the Inner islands. Macpherson stated it was a plentiful resident 'which often omits the latter part of its song on Skye'. Collier found it resident on Raasay but not plentiful. Baxter and Rintoul found it well distributed in suitable places in 1930 and a few pairs were apparently resident on Raasay in 1937. It was seen on Soay in 1952 by James Fisher.

It remained well distributed at the time of the 1968-72 *Atlas* with confirmed or probable breeding in 22 squares which probably led Thom to suggest that the species was widespread and common on Skye. Church and Lodge however, only found 1 pair on Raasay in 1982. It was recorded in only 5 squares during the 1981-83 *Winter Atlas*, which might indicate the first evidence of decline. There was a further and dramatic decline in records of this species during the 1988-91 breeding survey when the species had apparently disappeared from at least 16 squares. Similar declines were experienced in other parts of Scotland and Ireland. In earlier evidence of this decline Reed (1978) had attributed this decrease to agricultural changes and changes in human crofting populations.

Though the Garden Wildlife Survey of 2003 suggests it was recorded in 16% of gardens in South Skye, this is likely to also include historical data. A few pairs still appear to be present in the Aird of Sleat (Pat Newman pers comm.) up until 2004 but only occasional single birds have been recorded since. The Yellowhammer has suffered a significant decline in the last 20 years, and as a species which is largely sedentary, it is highly unlikely that it will ever recolonise many of its former haunts. Most sadly however, for a species which was at one time so much part of the crofting way of life, its virtual disappearance has largely gone unnoticed.

REED BUNTING   *Emberiza schoeniclus*   Gealag lòin (gealag dhubhchreannach)

Uncommon breeding resident.   **Red list species.**

It was 'Resident, and not uncommon in marshy situations' according to Macpherson in the *The Fauna*. Collier found it uncommon but breeding in suitable locations although it seemed to be absent in winter. Baxter & Rintoul found it 'very common at Loch Cill Chriosd and here and there elsewhere, where conditions are suitable'. It was apparently resident in small numbers on Raasay in 1937. During a winter visit to Pabay in 1956 Henson caught and ringed 17 birds, which gives an indication of the size of the population. Henson wrote:

> The Reed Bunting replaced the House Sparrow on Pabay. They fed in the farmyard and around the house, sitting cheeping on the roofs of buildings.

The species was well distributed at the time of the 1968-72 *Atlas* with confirmed or probable breeding in 22 squares. However, by the time of the 1981-83 *Winter Atlas*, it was only recorded in 8 squares. Skye certainly seems to have experienced a population crash by the time of the 1988-91 breeding survey, the species being absent from 13 squares where it formerly bred. Again this pattern is reflected elsewhere in the Highlands, and in the country generally which has resulted in its 'Red' status.

The Reed Bunting is now an uncommon breeding bird on Skye. It seems to be recorded more regularly in autumn and winter, usually in small numbers. Some time ago Pete Ellis recorded flocks of 30 on 15.10.1978 and 40 on 16.2.1979 at Aird Bernisdale which are the most significant flocks recorded in the last 25 years. On a more optimistic note the author also recorded a flock of 20+ at Aird Bernisdale on 30.10.2003, by far the best count in recent years. This might suggest that 2003 was a good breeding season which may be timely. There were 8 pairs at Loch Chaluim Chille, Kilmuir in May 2008. Given that this species is sedentary it will take the population some time to recover to its former level.

CORN BUNTING   *Emberiza calandra*   Gealag bhuachair

Bred formerly in small numbers. No recent records. Red list species.

It was regarded by Macpherson in *The Fauna* as a numerous resident: 'here in the north the songs of the Mavis and Corn Bunting enliven us throughout our long but usually open winters in the Hebrides'. In 1930 Baxter & Rintoul found it common about Staffin but only irregularly distributed elsewhere. On Raasay it was found by Collier to be extremely abundant between 1896 and 1902 but seems to have disappeared by the 1930s.

During the 1968-72 *Breeding Atlas* it was recorded as probably breeding in only a single square in north-west Skye. Again agricultural changes and crofting practices were regarded as causal factors of decline (Reed 1978). There was no record during the 1981-83 *Winter Atlas*. Thom suggested it last bred in Skye in 1970. Reed *et al.* regarded the species as recently extinct on Skye in 1983. However, it still appeared to have a toehold during the 1988-91 *Breeding Atlas*, being recorded in 2 squares.

Despite the later record above, it was reasonable to assume that the Corn Bunting has been extinct as a breeding species on Skye for 25 years until a singing bird was present at Lusta, Waternish from 26.6-9.7.2005.

ESCAPES

BLACK SWAN   *Cygnus atratus*

Vagrant.

A single bird, presumably an escapee, arrived at Loch Mòr, Waterstein on 3.4.2007 and remained until early September.

BIBLIOGRAPHY

Alexander, W. B., 1945. Woodcock in the British Isles. *Ibis* 512.

Baxter, Evelyn V. & Rintoul, Leonara Jeffrey. 1928. *The Geographical Distribution and Status of Birds in Scotland.* Oliver & Boyd, Edinburgh.

Baxter, Evelyn V. & Rintoul, Leonara Jeffrey. 1953. *The Birds of Scotland.* Oliver & Boyd, Edinburgh.

Benn, S., Burton, C. A., Tasker, M. L., Webb, A. & Ward, R. M. 1988. *Seabird distribution on the north-west Scottish shelf.* Nature Conservancy Council Chief Scientist Directorate Report No. 803.

Berry, Dr. John. 1939. *The status and distribution of Wild Geese and Wild Duck in Scotland.*

Boswell, James. 1746. *The Journal of a tour to the Hebrides with Samuel Johnson.* Charles Dilly, London.

Bromham, Janet. 2003. *The Skye & Lochalsh Biodiversity Action Plan.* The Highland Council, Inverness.

Burton, C.A., Tasker,M.L., Benn, S., Webb,A. & Leaper, G.M. 1986. *The Distribution of Seabirds off the North West coast of Scotland.* Nature Conservancy Council Chief Scientist Report No. 758.

Celoria, Francis. 2001. *The Rev. Hugh Alexander Macpherson : A life and a Bibliography.* Unpublished manuscript for Tullie House Museum, Carlisle.

Church, Tony & Lodge, Dave. 1982. *Raasay Bird Report.* Unpublished.

Collier, Charles. 1904. The Birds of the Island of Raasay. *Ibis*, pp. 490-513.

Cooper, Derek. 1970. *Skye.* Routledge & Kegan Paul Ltd., London.

Cramp, Stanley., Bourne, W. R. P. & Saunders, David. *The Seabirds of Britain and Ireland.* Collins, London.

Crane, Ken & Nellist, Kate. 1999. *Island Eagles.* Cartwheeling Press, Skye.

Darling, F. Fraser & Boyd, J. M. 1969. *The Highlands and Islands.* London.

Donald, C. 2000. Post breeding concentrations of adult Black-throated Divers in Wester Ross. *Scottish Birds.* Vol.21 No.1 pp 47-48.

Eagle, Raymond. 1991. *Seton Gordon: The Life and Times of a Highland Gentleman.* Lochar Publishing Ltd., Moffat.

Ellis, Peter. 1979. *Survey of Winter Birds on the Coast of Skye.* Unpublished NCC report.

Fox., A. D., Norriss, D. W., Stroud, D. A., Wilson, H. J. & Merne, O. J. 1998. The Greenland White-fronted Goose *Anser albifrons flavirostris* in Ireland and Britain 1982/83 – 1994/95. *Wildlife Biology* 4: 1-12.

Fox, Anthony D., 2003. *The Greenland White-fronted Goose.* Ph.D dissertation, National Environmental Research Institute, Denmark.

Garvie, Ellen I. 1999. *Gaelic names of Plants, Fungi & Animals.* Sabhal Mor Ostaig, Skye.

Gibbons, David Wingfield, Reid, James B. & Chapman, Robert A. 1993. *A New Atlas of Breeding Birds in Britain and Ireland: 1988-1991.* T. & A. D. Poyser, London.

Gordon, Seton. 1929. *The Charm of Skye.* Cassell and Company Ltd.

Gordon, Seton. 1931. *In the Highlands.* Cassell & Company Ltd.

Gordon, Seton. 1938. *Wild Birds in Britain.* Cassell & Company Ltd.

Gordon, Seton. 1955. *The Golden Eagle.* Collins, London.

Gray, Robert. 1871. *The Birds of the West of Scotland.* Thomas Murray & Son, Glasgow.

Harvie-Brown, J. A. & Macpherson, Rev. H. A. 1904. *A Vertebrate Fauna of Scotland: North-West Highlands and Skye.* David Douglas, Edinburgh.

Henson, N. 1956. Winter Birds on the Island of Pabbay, Skye. *The Glasgow Bird Bulletin,* Vol. 5 No. 3.

Highland Bird Report 1984-1999; 2002-2006. Annual Reports produced by the Highland Recorder.

Highland Raptor Study Group Reports. Annual report published until 2002.

Hope, Linnaes E. 1912. H. A. Macpherson MBOU: A memoir. *Transactions of the Carlisle Natural History Society,* Vol. 11.

Knowlton, Derek. 1977. *The Naturalist in the Hebrides.* David & Charles, London.

168

Lack, Peter. 1986. *The Atlas of Wintering Birds in Britain and Ireland.* T. & A. D. Poyser, London.

Lister-Kaye, John. 1972. *The White Island.* Longman, London.

Lloyd, Clare, Tasker, Mark. L. & Partidge, Ken 1991. *The Status of Seabirds in Britain and Ireland.* T. & A. D. Poyser, London.

Love, John A. 1983. *The Return of the Sea Eagle.* Cambridge University Press.

MacGillivray, William. 1837. *A History of British Birds.* Scott, Webster & Geary, London.

Macpherson, Rev. H. A. 1882. Rough Notes in Skye and Eigg. *The Zoologist,* 3rd Series, Vol. VI No. 71, pp. 418-423.

Macpherson, Rev. H. A. 1886. The Birds of Skye, with special reference to the Parish of Duirinish, Part 1. *Proceedings of the Royal Physical Society of Edinburgh,* Vol. 9, pp. 118-143.

Macpherson, Rev. H. A. 1886. Black-headed Gull and Common Scoter in Skye. *The Zoologist,* 3rd Series, Vol. X No. 120, p. 488.

Macpherson, Rev. H. A. 1889. Uncommon Birds in Skye. *The Zoologist,* 3rd Series, Vol. XIII No. 151, pp. 268-269.

Martin, Martin. 1703. *A description of the Western Isles of Scotland circa 1695.* Andrew Bell, London.

McMillan, R. 2005. Windfarms and Eagles - a case study of Edinbane, Skye. *Scottish Bird News* No. 75.

Mitchell, P. Ian, Newton, Stephen. F., Ratcliffe, Norman & Dunn, Timothy E. 2004. *Seabird Populations of Britain and Ireland: results of the Seabird 2000 census (1998-2002).* T. & A. D. Poyser, London.

Moser, M.E., Broad. R.A., Dennis, R.H. & Madders, M. 1986. The distribution and abundance of some coastal birds on the west and north-west coasts of Scotland in winter. *Scottish Birds,* Vol.14 Part 2, pp 61-67.

Murray, Iain M. 1954. Notes on the Birds of Skye. *The Glasgow and West of Scotland Bird Bulletin,* Vol. 3 No.1, pp. 6-12.

Nethersole-Thompson, Desmond. 1966. *The Snow Bunting.* Oliver & Boyd, Edinburgh.

New Statistical Account of Scotland, The. 1834-45.

Ogilvie, M. A. & Atkinson-Willes, G. L. 1983. Wildfowl in the Inner Hebrides. *Proceedings of the Royal Society of Edinburgh*, 83B, pp. 491-504.

Pennant, T. 1776. *A tour of Scotland, and Voyage to the Outer Hebrides, 1771 to 1776.*

Perry, Richard. 1944. *I went a Shepherding.* Lindsay Drummond Ltd., London.

Phillips, John. 2004. *Isles of Skye and Raasay Garden Wildlife Survey 2003.* The Highland Council Ranger Service.

Ratcliffe, D. A. 1976. Observations on the breeding of the Golden Plover in Great Britain. *Bird Study* 23, pp. 63-116.

Ratcliffe, Derek. 1993 (2nd edn.). *The Peregrine Falcon.* T. & A. D. Poyser, London.

Reed, T. M., Currie, A. & Love, J. A. 1983. Birds of the Inner Hebrides. *Proceedings of the Royal Society of Edinburgh*, 83B, pp. 449-472.

Richmond, W. Kenneth. 1968. *A regional guide to the birds of Scotland.* Constable & Co. Ltd., London.

Scottish Bird Report. Annual species report of the Scottish Ornithologists' Club 1968-2001.

Sharrock, J. T. R. 1976. *The Atlas of Breeding Birds in Britain and Ireland.* T. & A. D. Poyser, London.

Sillar, Frederick C. & Meyler, Ruth M. 1973. *Skye.* David & Charles, Newton Abbot.

Statistical Account of Scotland. 1791-1799.

Temperley, George. W. 1938. *The Birds of Raasay. Notes of the Bird Life of the Island of Raasay, Inner Hebrides.* Reprinted from *The Scottish Naturalist.* 27pp.

Thom, Valerie M. 1986. *Birds in Scotland.* T. & A .D. Poyser

Wernham, Chris, Toms, Mike, Marchant, John, Clark, Jacquie, Siriwardena, Gavin & Baillie, Stephen (eds.). 2002. *The Migration Atlas.* T. & A. D. Poyser, London.

INDEX BY COMMON AND BOU NAME

NOTES

www.skye-birds.com

The objectives of this website are to:

- highlight the wide variety of birds which can be seen and where to see them
- encourage locals and visitors to record their bird observations
- stimulate involvement in fieldwork
- contribute to the conservation and protection of a number of rare and spectacular birds so that future generations can enjoy birding, against the most dramatic backdrop in Britain.

The website also offers the following services:

- Details of walks, talks and wildlife related events on the island of Skye and neighbouring Lochalsh.
- Information on any ongoing wildlife surveys
- A Gallery of outstanding images taken in the area by local photographers as well as photographs from birding trips in Europe and elsewhere.
- **www.skye-birds.com** acts as a publisher in its own right and has produced several papers as well as Skye Birds.
- We provide self-catering accommodation for up to 6 in a spectacular location in the village of Elgol.
- Most ornithological survey work is carried out in a voluntary capacity but we are also in a position to undertake limited commissioned consultancy work using established methodologies.
- Guiding – we provide assistance with guided walks and tours outwith the main breeding season or in circumstances which will not compromise the breeding locations of our rarer birds.